Complete Conditioning for
GOLF

Pete Draovitch, MS, ACT, PT

Wayne Westcott, PhD, CSCS

Human Kinetics

Library of Congress Cataloging-in-Publication Data

Draovitch, Pete, 1961-
    Complete conditioning for golf / Pete Draovitch, Wayne L. Westcott.
      p.   cm.
    ISBN 0-88011-986-1
    1. Golf--Training.   I. Westcott, Wayne L., 1949- . II. Title.
    GV979.T68D73   1999
    613.7'4--dc21   99-24207
                                                  CIP

    ISBN: 0-88011-986-6

Developmental Editor: Julie Rhoda; **Assistant Editor:** Sandra Merz Bott; **Copyeditor:** Stephen Moore; **Proofreader:** Sarah Wiseman; **Graphic Designer:** Stuart Cartwright; **Graphic Artist:** Kimberly Maxey; **Photo Editor:** Clark Brooks; **Cover Designer:** Jack Davis; **Photographer (cover):** © Matthew Harris/The Golf Picture Library; **Photographer (interior):** Sharon Townson (pp. 63-87) and Linda Kaye (all other photos unless otherwise noted); **Illustrators:** Beth Young, Kimberly Maxey; **Printer:** Versa Press

Human Kinetics books are available at special discounts for bulk purchase. Special editions or book excerpts can also be created to specification. For details, contact the Special Sales Manager at Human Kinetics.

Printed in the United States of America   10 9 8 7 6 5 4 3 2 1

Web site: http://www.humankinetics.com/

United States: Human Kinetics
P.O. Box 5076
Champaign, IL 61825-5076
1-800-747-4457
e-mail: humank@hkusa.com

Canada: Human Kinetics
475 Devonshire Road Unit 100
Windsor, ON N8Y 2L5
1-800-465-7301 (in Canada only)
e-mail: humank@hkcanada.com

Europe: Human Kinetics, P.O. Box IW14
Leeds LS16 6TR, United Kingdom
+44 (0)113-278 1708
e-mail: humank@hkeurope.com

Australia: Human Kinetics
57A Price Avenue
Lower Mitcham, South Australia
5062
(08) 82771555
e-mail: humank@hkaustralia.com

New Zealand: Human Kinetics
P.O. Box 105-231, Auckland Central
09-523-3462
e-mail: humank@hknewz.com

To Greg and Laura Norman for exposing me to this wonderful, but sometimes crazy, game of golf; to my patients who continually challenge me; and to my family, especially my wife, Debra, and daughter, Victoria Morgan, who unconditionally offer me support, balance, laughter, love, in a world that sometimes moves way too fast.

—Pete Draovitch

CONTENTS

FOREWORD

I have been playing golf for more than half my life and have always held the belief that a sound body leads to a sound mind. I am so committed to this philosophy that six years ago I hired my own personal physical therapist to oversee my strength, conditioning, and rehabilitation program. Programs for recreational and tour level players certainly differ, but the goal of any program should be the same: to change the composition and reaction ability of one's neuromuscular system in order to develop a more consistent golf swing.

Over the years, technological advances have led to incredible changes to the game of golf. Yet not until recently has attention been paid to how changing your physiology will improve your game. Regardless of your talent level, available time, or level of fitness, this book provides you with options for undertaking an effective program that will help you correct problematic neuromuscular imbalances. And by following these proven programs, you are sure to improve your game.

—Greg Norman

ACKNOWLEDGMENTS

This is our favorite page of the book, as we greatly appreciate the invaluable assistance offered by the following individuals in producing this text. First we are most grateful to the helpful editors at Human Kinetics, especially Ted Miller, Julie Rhoda, and Sandra Merz Bott. Next we want to thank our photographers, Sharon Townson and Linda Kaye, and our exercise models, T. Ross Bailey, Jane Bowler, Bill Johnson, Laura Prisco, members of TCU Athletics, Scott Volpitto, and Ralph Yohe, for their excellent work in presenting the visual content of this book. We are also indebted to Steve McGee and Gray Cook who reviewed the initial manuscript; CDM Medical for allowing us to use their XTS tubing system and BackSystem 3; Paul Hospenthal, PT, for his input regarding physical limitations and swing compensations; and Debra Wein, MS, RD, for her insight concerning the nutritional aspects of golf conditioning. In addition, we would like to thank Chris Welch for his biomechanical contributions and his help in formulating easy-to-understand drills and exercises. We highly commend our administrative assistants, Christy Blaha and Susan Ramsden, for the many hours they spent typing and reworking our manuscript. Most of all we appreciate our wives, Debra Draovitch and Claudia Westcott, as well as God's grace for enabling us to complete this writing project.

INTRODUCTION

Golf is a great game enjoyed by more than 25 million Americans. You are undoubtedly one of that number, and whether you're a tournament player or novice, you certainly want to perform as well as you can. You also want to avoid injuries and physical setbacks that can easily detract from your golf experiences. The purpose of this book is to present a sensible and personal physical conditioning program that will enhance your playing ability and reduce your injury risk. As you will see, these desirable outcomes are two sides of the conditioning coin, and the same training program that increases your driving power also decreases your injury potential.

The golf swing is a complex, explosive, and physically stressful action, and you must prepare your body to both produce and withstand the forces required for powerful drives. You can improve several important aspects of your swing through functional fitness training that should significantly increase your driving distance.

1. You can increase your club swing range by improving your joint flexibility.

2. You can increase your club swing speed by developing your muscle strength.

3. You can increase your club swing power by training your dynamic postural balance and segmental coordination.

Improving your golf game through better physical fitness is what this book is all about. Of course, this includes cardiovascular activity and appropriate nutrition, which we address in detail in chapter 7. Our primary focus, however, is on safe, sensible, effective and efficient exercise programs designed specifically for golfers. These progressive fitness components include *flexibility for full swing mechanics* (chapter 3); *strength for maximum distance and control* (chapter 4); *postural stability for a consistent swing plane* (chapter 5); *coordination for power transfer and skill execution* (chapter 6); and the *complete golf conditioning program* (chapter 8).

Because we want you to fully understand the fitness essentials for optimum golf and how to evaluate your personal fitness strengths and weaknesses relevant to golf performance, we devote the first two chapters to these topics. After following the suggested exercise programs and developing a functional level of golf fitness, you will find it relatively easy to maintain your new physical abilities. For this reason, we conclude the book with our *15-minute golf fitness workout* (chapter 9), which enables you to train productively even when time is limited.

We believe that the first step for improving your golf game and avoiding physical setbacks is a sound general exercise program that increases your overall fitness. The second step is more targeted training that includes specific stretching, strengthening, and sequencing exercises to enhance your power production and elevate your playing ability to higher performance levels. This book presents well-tested programs of basic exercise and sport-specific training known as the PAC (Progressive Adaptive Conditioning) Total Golf system which can increase your driving distance, injury resistance, and playing enjoyment.

CHAPTER 1

FITNESS ESSENTIALS FOR GOLF

Is golf ready for fitness? Yes! What

was once the exception is becoming the rule, especially as we see the success of motivated, talented players who practice fitness training. These players value physical fitness so much that an exercise trailer and full-time training and rehabilitative staff are now available for players at all USPGA events. Most of these exercise trailers are equipped with a Versaclimber, stationary bicycle, and Frankenslide slide board for aerobic conditioning. A single multistation resistance machine and a variety of dumbbells, medicine balls, and rehabilitation equipment round out the strength training options. Many exercise programs could be designed to use the golfer's own body weight, elastic tubing, and stabilization balls, however.

The staff is composed largely of physical therapists, but physicians and chiropractors also play active roles in the system. The physical therapists work long hours to provide the players with the expertise and knowledge to keep them on the course for improved physical performance and reduced injury risk.

Today's physically fit players appreciate the USPGA's trailers at tournaments. In fact, we're aware of one instance when the trailer was not available for a European Tour event and at least one well-known player withdrew from the tournament. The trailer is a means for some participants to get through a long and demanding competitive season; the exercise trailer provides an important source of physical and mental stability for golfers at the highest level of a tedious and technical sport.

Golf is a game in which a small advantage in one area can mean the difference between finishing 1st or finishing 20th. Scan the pro tour statistics and you will see the difference between a person ranking 1st in the category and 25th or 30th could be as small as a quarter of a shot difference in scoring average. Multiplying that by four per round, however, shows that a small edge allows a player to win by one shot instead of losing by one shot. The other advantage to being fit is that when the body feels and functions well, the mind is more able to focus on the task at hand: the next shot.

History has shown that most golfers are not willing to spend a great deal of time working out, even if it improves their games. For this reason, golf conditioning programs should be efficient and address the areas where they will most benefit performance and reduce injuries. We must remember that not too long ago, other competitive sports arenas placed little or no emphasis on muscular development. In the 1960s, for example, few football teams participated in off-season strength training programs. Today, players require year-round strength training just to stay competitive. In the 1970s, basketball players were told to stay out of the weight room because strong muscles were incompatible with shooting ability. Now basketball players continue their strength training on a year-round basis. In the 1980s the Oakland A's won two World Series with strength-trained athletes such as Jose Canseco and Mark McGwire—big, strong, powerful men who hit many home runs during those championship years. It was not long afterward that strength training became accepted practice in the baseball community.

We firmly believe that it is only a matter of time before golfers, too, recognize the necessity of physical conditioning. The new breed of player and the body type you see on the professional tour are indicative of what is happening in golf. The top young players are leaner, more muscular, and more flexible than the generation of golfers before them.

This fitness training can reduce your physical limitations and help you optimize your swing pattern. Training enables more efficient transfer of momentum, which translates into improved ball striking capability and increased club head speed at impact.

A theoretical model has been created to compare baseball energy requirements to golf energy requirements. According to this construct, the amount of energy transferred to a golf ball hit 300 yards is of about the same magnitude as the energy transferred to a baseball hit 300 feet from a resting position. Consider that a 10-handicap golfer will take about 50 hard swings and another 50 to 75 practice swings, per round, with a club that weighs slightly less than a baseball bat. If you compare this golfer to the baseball player who bats five times during a game and takes about 15 total swings, it is easy to see a difference in swinging requirements. Furthermore, golfers walk about 8,000 yards per round; a center fielder travels less than 2,000 yards, moving back and forth to the dugout between innings. Even including movements to run base paths or chase down fly balls, the total distance traveled by a baseball player does not come close to that traveled by a golfer. The conclusion is that though golf may require less intensity than baseball, the greater volume of activity provides higher overall energy costs when compared to baseball. The baseball community having accepted physical training as part of its program, we are confident that golfers soon will follow suit.

Is your fitness level appropriate for high-performance golf?

IMPROVE YOUR FITNESS—IMPROVE YOUR GAME

Being physically fit allows you to walk 18 holes of golf without feeling fatigued and to stay focused throughout the game. Perhaps more important, a well-conditioned body can produce more powerful and coordinated swinging actions that result in longer and better-placed drives. Higher fitness levels also reduce your recovery time, thereby letting you enjoy more frequent rounds of golf.

The repetitive nature of the golf swing predisposes both professional and amateur golfers to injury. To avoid or limit physical breakdown, we encourage a preventive program of physical conditioning. The first steps are to recognize your own physical limitations and understand what you must do to strengthen these weaknesses. If left unattended, they certainly will lead to eventual breakdown. This is why it is imperative to become aware of potential problems and preventive measures. A successful training program should address cardiorespiratory endurance, postural imbalances, golf-specific strength, functional flexibility, balance, and motor learning.

SWING SEQUENCE

Because the golf swing is one of the most unnatural, complex, and explosive movements in sport, you must prepare your body to perform this powerful athletic action as successfully and safely as possible. Better joint flexibility lets you swing in a fluid manner through a full range of movement. Greater muscular strength provides more striking force to drive the ball farther. Enhanced balance and coordination are the keys to control and will help you place each shot closer to your target area. Taken together, these fitness factors can make a big difference in your golf performance, playing satisfaction, and game scores.

© Action Images

Se Ri Pak, winner of two major championships in 1998.

Elements of a Golf Swing

The American Sports Medicine Institute (ASMI) in Birmingham, Alabama, breaks down the golf swing into five separate biomechanical phases or positions that are useful for designing a sport-specific program for golf:

Set-up
Backswing
Transition
Downswing
Follow-through

Chris Welch, president of Human Performance Technologies of Jupiter, Florida, uses his program and software package—the Biolink System—to analyze the golf swing using body segments (hips, trunk, shoulders, and arms) organized into functional links (hips-trunk, trunk-shoulders, and shoulders-arms). The main purpose of the Biolink System is to determine specific forces and power outputs during the swing phases and how these factors relate to optimal club head speed. The analysis allows you to determine objectively how your power might be leaking away.

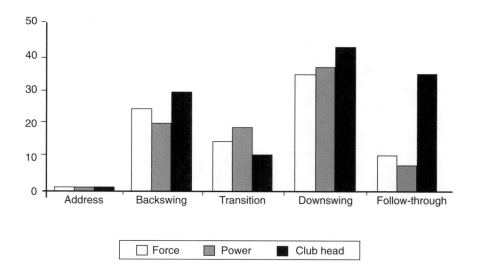

The power output of the five biomechanical phases of a golf swing.

The forces that act on the segmental components of the spine vary from individual to individual, depending on skill level and physiological factors. Preexisting conditions of the spine, such as degenerative joint disease, postural imbalance, or degenerative disc disease, will change the way swinging forces are distributed. Of course, if the physical demands exceed tissue function or recovery capabilities, the result will be a breakdown of the joint structure. Normal forces that occur to the spine during the golf swing are as follows:

Anterior and posterior sliding forces between the segments (shear forces)

Lateral bending forces between the segments

Twisting (torsional) forces between the segments

Compressive forces between the segments

Recent research at the New Jersey School of Medicine has found that professional golfers demonstrate less sliding, lateral bending, and twisting forces than amateur golfers. Compressive forces were approximately eight times body weight for both groups. Neuromuscular firing of the trunk muscles revealed that professionals use less effort while performing the trunk coiling and uncoiling process. In addition, the sequence of neuromuscular firing was different between the groups. These findings suggest that the lower-handicapped golfers have more efficient swing patterns than higher-handicapped golfers. The key in explaining the way that these spinal segments and muscular forces are decreased in the better golfer might lie in how well each individual is able to pass momentum from one segment of the body to another.

This efficient passing of momentum, commonly referred to as *kinetic linking*, can be improved through training. By increasing muscle strength, while at the same time improving joint flexibility, balance, and coordination, you will develop more efficient and effective summation of momentum. This basically translates into increased club head speed at impact, which results in longer drives.

Golf Swing Analysis

Kinesiologically, much of the work on golf swing analysis has been performed at the biomechanics laboratory at Tenent Medical Center in Englewood, California. Most of this work has been done under the supervision of sports medicine pioneer physician Frank Jobe. The analyses show that there is little activity of the trunk muscles during the backswing and relatively high and constant activity in these muscles throughout the remainder of the swing.

These results demonstrate the importance of the trunk musculature throughout the golfer's entire performance enhancement, preventive, and rehabilitative program. Studies of the shoulder demonstrated that the rotator cuff muscles acted predominantly at the end ranges of motion. The internal shoulder rotators were activated during acceleration and the front shoulder muscles were activated during the swing and follow-through movements. The middle and rear shoulder muscles on the lead arm were extremely active to stabilize the shoulder girdle throughout the swing. More important, peak muscle activity of the hip and knee during the golf swing was recorded before the peak muscle activity of the trunk and shoulders region. This substantiates the importance of the sequential actions of the different components of the body for generating power.

To obtain the greatest benefit from proper sequencing of swinging actions, you must have strong leg, thigh, and hip muscles to generate driving power. These lower-body forces then must be transferred through well-conditioned midsection muscles to the upper body. Strong chest, back, and shoulder muscles permit greater acceleration of the club, while maintaining control through trained arms and forearms. There is perhaps no single action in sport that requires more overall muscular strength, joint flexibility, and movement coordination than a perfectly executed golf swing.

CARDIORESPIRATORY ENDURANCE

Cardiorespiratory endurance is a good indicator of overall physical capacity, especially the ability to do more work, burn more calories, and recover better from activity bouts such as a round of golf. Although many golf courses require you to use a cart, several hours of play can leave you feeling quite fatigued on the last few holes. If you walk (which we strongly recommend whenever possible), you are likely to suffer an even greater performance decrement unless you have a moderately high level of cardiorespiratory fitness. Playing golf, unfortunately, is not the best means for getting in better shape to play better golf. Instead, you will make much greater progress by specifically conditioning your cardiorespiratory system.

Usually called *aerobic conditioning*, this aspect of your exercise program requires about 20 to 30 minutes of moderate activity, three days a week.

Walking, jogging, stepping, and cycling are all appropriate activities for improving cardiorespiratory fitness. The level of conditioning is closely related to the intensity of the exercise. For example, a slow walk that raises your heart rate only 20 beats per minute above its resting level (typically about 70 beats per minute) is unlikely to have much impact on your aerobic capacity. A fast walk or jog, however, one that elevates your heart rate 60 beats per minute above resting, should have significant conditioning benefit. Performed on a regular basis, 20 to 30 minutes of moderate aerobic activity should make your heart a stronger pump, your circulatory system a more efficient blood transporter, and your blood cells better carriers of oxygen.

A simple formula for selecting appropriate exercise intensity is to train at about 70 percent of your estimated maximum heart rate. You can easily approximate this by subtracting your age from 220, and exercising hard enough that your heart rate is about 70 percent of this number.

Estimating Your Maximum Heart Rate

John is 50 years old. His estimated maximum heart rate is therefore 170 beats per minute (220 – 50 = 170). To attain cardiorespiratory conditioning benefits efficiently, John should perform aerobic activity (walking, jogging, stepping, cycling, etc.) at an intensity that raises his heart rate to about 120 beats per minute. Of course, this is just an approximation. If this level of training feels hard, it should be reduced; if this level of training feels easy, it should be increased. General age-related maximum heart rates and the 70 percent cardiorespiratory training levels are presented in table 1.1.

Table 1.1   Heart Rate Table for Cardiorespiratory Fitness

Age (years)	15	25	35	45	55	65	75	85
Maximum heart rate (bpm)	205	195	185	175	165	155	145	135
70% training heart rate (bpm)	144	137	130	123	116	109	102	95

FUNCTIONAL FLEXIBILITY

Flexibility is the one component of fitness that has been appreciated by golfers for many years. By enhancing joint flexibility you can lengthen your golf swing and increase your club head speed. Your joint flexibility is determined by your movement ability and dictates the safe ranges for your swing patterns. It is important to note that excellent flexibility alone does not guarantee a good golf swing. Inability to sequence movements at proper times may result in reaching maximum club head speed well before impact, with a related loss of power and reduced driving distance.

GOLF-SPECIFIC STRENGTH

The strengthening program for golf should include work for the trunk, as well as for the muscles of the upper and lower body. Because the golf swing is not a simple, linear motion, you should implement an integrated, multijoint strengthening program. Remember that your hips and legs produce most of the force for a powerful golf swing. This momentum must be transferred through a stable trunk to the upper body, which simultaneously delivers and counteracts the forceful striking action of the club. A successful swing, therefore, requires sufficient strength and coordinated actions among the major muscles that make up these different body segments. Of course, strong muscles also are essential for proper posture, which assures consistent swing deliveries and a stable head that maintains uninterrupted eye focus on the golf ball.

Postural Balance

Postural balance is an important component of your golf game. Unfortunately, physical activities such as golf, in which one side of the body is used differently than the other side of the body, tend to promote postural imbalances that can impede performance and cause injury. It is important to determine whether the postural imbalance is a normal response to sport mechanics, however, or whether it is due to pathological conditions. A solid golf conditioning program strives for front-to-back and left-to-right body balance. Although this may never be fully achieved because of the sport mechanics, it always should remain a primary goal of your golf conditioning program.

LPGA Hall of Fame member, Nancy Lopez.

Balance represents a complex neuromuscular communication system. It relies on feedback from the central nervous system, the eyes, the inner ear, and tiny message receptors in the joints and soft tissues. Balance is necessary in maintaining appropriate spine (trunk and torso) positions throughout the swing. If balance is not maintained during the swinging action, shoulder turn, weight shift, and force transfer may be affected and the shot outcome will be compromised. As one grows older, the sensory organs and balance systems become less sensitive. It therefore might be advantageous to actually make better postural balance one of the primary parts of a conditioning program.

MOTOR LEARNING

Motor learning is simply teaching the neuromuscular system to perform a specific task in a consistent, reproducible fashion. Because the golf swing requires communication among all body segments, motor learning or muscle memory might be a key factor for further improvement. Several motor learning adaptations must occur for your body to become more functionally efficient, therefore enhancing your golf performance and reducing injury risk. You must teach your body parts to work correctly and sequentially, within the available range of motion for your golf swing.

The goal of motor learning, or computer-like programming of the neuromuscular system, is to develop the least stressful and most productive movement patterns for a successful golf swing. Remember that movement can be defined as a series of muscular contractions, controlled by the nervous system and conditioned through the process of motor learning.

NUTRITION

Although most people do not consider golf to be an activity that requires power eating or a special diet, proper nutrition is certainly an important component of a golf conditioning program. After all, appropriate eating patterns are necessary to maintain high energy levels throughout a four-hour athletic event. In addition, golfers involved in physical conditioning activities require better nutrition to maximize their fitness development.

Eating for good health is step one because it applies to all areas of life. Eating for improved golf performance is step two, because sustained energy levels can make a big difference in your playing ability, especially on the back nine.

Our recommended nutrition program is sound and sensible, and completely consistent with the United States Department of Agriculture Food Guide Pyramid. We do emphasize eating appropriate carbohydrate foods for supplying and sustaining elevated energy levels throughout your golf game.

THE NEXT STEP

An effective golf training program serves a dual purpose: to improve performance and reduce the risk of injury. Many recreational golfers experience back, hip, elbow, and shoulder injuries that might be preventable. It therefore makes perfect sense that golfers can benefit greatly from a training program that conditions these vulnerable parts of the body. Our objective is to educate golfers regarding the potentially harmful forces the golf swing places on an unconditioned or poorly prepared body. More important, we provide a training program in chapter 8 that should benefit every golfer, regardless of age, handicap, fitness level, schedule constraints, or any physical limitations.

CHAPTER 2

GOLF FITNESS EVALUATION

Although it took some time, even Jack Nicklaus recognized his need to attain better physical condition to continue a successful competitive career. It was only right after the 1986 Masters that he realized the importance of an exercise program to help him maintain a competitive edge into the 1990s.

Assessing your present fitness level and following an appropriate conditioning program is an important step for improving your golf performance and raising your playing ability to a higher level. If you currently have injuries or are experiencing health problems, however, be sure to consult with your physician or medical specialist before taking the fitness evaluation.

Keep in mind also that symptoms in one area of the body can be caused by problems elsewhere. For example, Davis Love was treated for hip pain that was later determined to be caused by a back problem. In a similar situation, Jose Mario Olazabal labored with a foot problem for

© Action Images

Jack Nicklaus used an exercise program to avoid back surgery.

almost two years before further examination revealed that the pain was referred from the low back. Fortunately, once the real problem is identified and treated successfully, high-level golf play can be resumed. Improved physical fitness clearly is an important component in both the remediation and prevention of injury. So how do you begin the process?

If you have high playing aspirations, access to a team of golf pros, biomechanists, physicians, physical therapists, nutritionists, and exercise specialists obviously is an advantage for achieving your performance potential. Even working with a trained teaching professional can greatly enhance your golf success and satisfaction. In case you prefer a self-assessment, however, we have provided a relatively simple system for evaluating specific fitness and performance factors.

SWING SELF-EVALUATION

How often have you had difficulty reaching a swing position and then practiced various drills to try to correct the problem? If your backswing were short or didn't produce sufficient power, for example, you could find many remedial drills—but first you must identify the specific part of your body that is restricting your backswing.

For example, your backswing might be limited by tight rotator cuff (shoulder) muscles, tight hip joints and surrounding musculature, lack of coordination of the upper and lower body, restricted midspine motion, tight *latissimus dorsi* (upper back) muscles, and even restricted cervical (neck) muscles. Because there are so many possible causes, we recommend initial screening to better identify any areas of restriction. The next section will help you identify possible problem areas, which then can be trained appropriately for better results. If you currently are experiencing any musculoskeletal problems, however, we encourage you to see a physician or physical therapist first, preferably one who has expertise in spine and sports injuries.

SCREENING PROCEDURES

These basic screening assessments for mobility and stability address the components of flexibility, strength, balance, and coordination, and may provide invaluable information for enhancing your golf swing. Failure to identify general problems could lead to inconsistent swing patterns and poor performance. The screening procedures should expose significant structural, mechanical, and soft-tissue restrictive problems. They also should provide information for eliminating unproductive drills and for establishing training programs that are most likely to enhance your driving performance.

CARDIORESPIRATORY ENDURANCE

Although cardiorespiratory endurance is not directly related to golf performance, it does have an effect on your staying power for several quality hours on the links. Generally speaking, we recommend that you develop enough aerobic fitness to walk a mile in less than 16 minutes, and to walk two miles in less than 34 minutes. If you can do this with erect posture, long strides, fluid movement, and moderate effort, from a cardiorespiratory perspective you should be well-conditioned for golf.

FLEXIBILITY

UPPER BACK/HIP MOBILITY

Focus: Hip joint limitation may be observed by performing this assessment.

Procedure:

1. Perform a squat to a comfortable depth, keeping your heels flat on the floor.
2. Note whether one hip is higher than the other at the lowest point of the squat.
3. Stand up.

Assessment: Unless you are standing in front of a full-length mirror, you might not be able to assess your hip height accurately; but a good indicator is whether or not you feel your weight is being distributed equally on both feet.

HIP/ANKLE MOBILITY

Focus: Ankle joint limitations are assessed with this test.

Procedure:

1. Stand facing a waist high bar, holding onto the bar. (You may also do this assessment by standing in a doorway, facing one side, holding the door jamb.)

2. Squat and note whether there is a difference in your weight distribution on either the right or the left side of the body.

3. Once you have noted weight distributions, keep your heels flat on the floor and try to rock forward by bending your knees.

Assessment: If you are unable to rock forward, you might have restrictions within the ankle joint.

UPPER BACK MOBILITY

Focus: Restrictions in the *latissimus dorsi* (mid- and upper back) muscles can be discovered by doing this test.

Procedure:

1. From a standing position, raise your hands over your head and perform a squat.

2. Note the position of your arms in relation to your ear.

3. Now sit against a wall or door frame and lean forward as necessary to keep your lower back flat against the wall.

4. Raise your hands above your head.

5. Note the difference in your arm position when you were standing and when you were seated in the doorway.

Assessment: Changing the position of your lower back, neck, or pelvis can restrict shoulder elevation, because these areas serve as points of muscle attachment. If you are unable to achieve at least the same amount of elevation as you did when standing, then your upper and mid-back should be targeted in your training program.

STRENGTH AND STABILITY

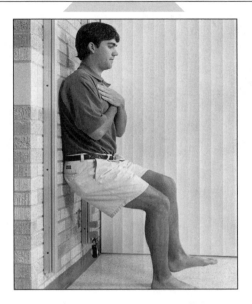

ABDOMINAL STRENGTH

Focus: Your spine and trunk should be stable during the golf swing. This test assesses strength in your abdominal muscles. Although the abdominal muscles can be considered as a single muscle group, different points of attachment suggest different roles in trunk stability.

Procedure:

1. Find a doorway or a flat wall.
2. Sit against the door frame or wall at a comfortable level.
3. Roll your pelvis backward until the lower back is in full contact with the door frame. Adjust your sitting level if necessary to make it easier to keep your back flat against the wall.
4. Keeping the back flat against the wall, lift one foot off the ground and hold it for approximately two seconds.
5. Repeat this procedure with the opposite foot.

Assessment: Inability to maintain the back flat against the door frame when lifting your foot indicates abdominal weakness. Be sure to have someone else observe your ability to stay flat against the door frame; you might not be able to perceive a change in your position.

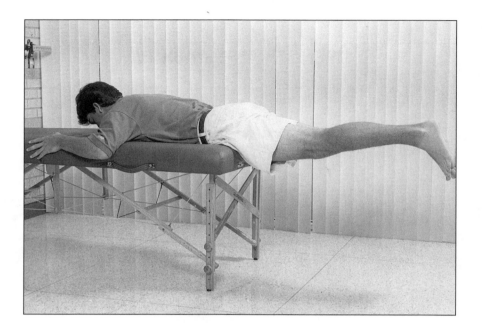

LOW BACK STRENGTH

Focus: This test assesses the strength of the hip extensors and low back muscles.

Procedure:

1. Lie face down on an exam table or over a stabilization ball such that your body is hanging off the table from the hips down.
2. Lift your legs so that your body is straight and parallel to the floor.
3. Hold this position for as long as possible.
4. Record your time (in seconds).

Assessment: If you have difficulty holding the horizontal position for at least 90 seconds, you are likely to benefit from a low back and hip extensor strengthening program. These tests should not take the place of a physical examination (if you have a recognizable problem), but might give you some indication about your trunk stability.

Tip: If you are extremely weak in the abdominal or low back muscles, do not proceed with further testing or training until you have strengthened these essential areas.

BALANCE AND COORDINATION

Balance and coordination are the final two components of a properly executed golf swing. The definition of coordination is simply the action of two or more joints in relation to one another to produce skilled movement. This is what we see in a properly executed golf swing. We assess these abilities with the *static balance test,* also known as the "stork stand."

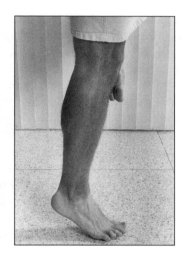

STATIC BALANCE TEST

Focus: This test assesses your balance while standing still.

Procedure:

1. Stand on one foot (first your backswing leg and then your follow-through leg).
2. Place the foot of the untested leg against the lower part of the support leg.
3. Next, place your hands on your hips.
4. Slide the foot up the lower leg so that it rests just below the knee.
5. Raise the heel of the support foot from the floor and attempt to maintain balance for as long as possible. Do not remove your hands from the hips or allow your heel to touch the floor.
6. Record your best time (in seconds) out of three attempts.

Assessment: If you are unable to hold this position for at least 10 seconds on each leg, you need work on your balance.

FUNCTIONAL PERFORMANCE MODEL

The self-evaluation presented thus far serves only as a baseline. The recommended assessment process for professionals who make their living playing golf involves a comprehensive evaluation tool called the *functional performance model.* You will see that this is a rather complex process and that much communication is necessary among players and their conditioning coaches to further improve performance at the highest level.

The functional performance model serves as an accurate means of assessing areas where your swing mechanics might break down and where you might be experiencing power leaks. The functional performance model begins with a biomechanical analysis, followed by clinical, structural, and functional analyses. Depending on the outcome of the clinical evaluation, the professional golfer might be encouraged to see a physician or a physical therapist to begin a rehabilitation program, or to meet with a fitness professional to develop a personalized exercise program.

Such an exercise program is broken down into two different areas: the basic program for the golfer in reasonably good physical condition, and what we call the clinical program, for the person who might not be fit enough to do more advanced exercises. The clinical program basically addresses the functional areas of *mobility* and *stability.* If the assessment reveals a deficiency in general fitness level, a customized exercise program can be developed. We believe that all golf conditioning programs can benefit from the PAC Total Golf system, because it addresses sport-specific muscular strength, functional flexibility, dynamic postural balance, and segmental coordination. These four components are the key factors for performing correct and consistent golf swings.

DRIVING RANGE EVALUATION FORM

The driving range evaluation form helps to assess the individual fitness components of posture, balance stability, coordinated stability, and functional mobility. The evaluation process helps you to identify musculoskeletal limitations before signing up for swing lessons. A player who is unable to do a crossover step either to the right or left, for example, might be unable to complete the swing follow-through due to inadequate hip mobility. It also might mean that a compensating factor is going to occur in this player's backswing, one that will not allow proper loading or coiling to take place.

You and a friend might want to assess one another for these factors at the driving range before and after hitting balls. You do need someone to help be your eyes for this assessment. See the Driving Range Evaluation Form (below) for more information.

Driving Range Evaluation Form

Posture

In front of a mirror, evaluate your lower back posture from behind and from the side. Do you have a flat back? Are your buttocks tucked beneath your body? Or do you have a swayback, such that your buttocks stick out? If your posture does not exhibit these qualities, for the sake of this evaluation, you can consider your posture to be normal. Circle your exhibited posture:

Flat back   Swayback   Normal

If your posture is other than normal, focus particularly on the exercises presented in chapter 5 to improve your postural stability.

Balance and Stability

Single leg stance—Stand on your right leg first and evaluate how long you can hold your balance. A passing score is 10 seconds. Perform the trial 3 times on each leg or until you can stand for 10 seconds on each leg.

Single leg stance for 10 seconds:

yes   Right   no

yes   Left   no

Pelvic height—Check your pelvic height by having someone stand behind you and place their hands on the tops of each side of your hip bone. Your partner should be able to tell by placing his or her hands on your hips and viewing from eye level whether one hip is higher or lower than the other or if they are level. Record your findings:

Right hip is higher.   Right hip is lower.   Hips are level.

If you were unable to stand for more than 10 seconds on one leg or if your hips are not level, the exercises in chapter 5 can help you alleviate imbalances and improve your golf swing.

continued

Driving Range Evaluation Form *(continued)*

Coordinated Stability

Standing pelvic tilt—Get into your normal golf set-up stance and evaluate the position of your pelvis. Now slightly bend your knees and attempt to tilt your pelvis independently of the rest of your body by first moving it backward and then forward. If you are unable to do this without moving parts of your body other than your pelvis, you may be restricted by tight or weak musculature or an inability to coordinate the motion.

Were you able to tilt your pelvis (circle one)?

yes   no

Crossover step—While keeping your trunk facing straight ahead, take your left foot and cross it over your right foot. If you have to roll to the outside part of your planted foot or are unable to keep your planted foot firmly on the ground when crossing the other leg over, you may be prone to substituting other body movements during the backswing or during the follow through of your golf swing. Look to see that you don't rotate your body to achieve a foot flat position; this can tell you a lot about what is happening during your swing. Record your results by circling the correct response:

When your *right foot was planted*, did it roll to the outside or come off the ground when you crossed with your left leg?

yes   no

When your *left foot was planted*, did it roll to the outside or come off the ground when you crossed with your right leg?

yes   no

If you were unable to tilt your pelvis, emphasize incorporating the drills and exercises from chapters 3, 4, and 6 into your complete conditioning program.

Functional Mobility

Elevated side bending—Stand with your feet shoulder-width apart. Grasp a club with both hands and extend your arms over your head. Place your right foot behind your left foot. Allow the right foot or hip to move to the right and then bend to your left side, being sure to only move from the trunk. Finally, use your left arm to pull your right arm over the top of your head. By sequencing this movement from the hip to the trunk to the arm you can see where

Driving Range Evaluation Form *(continued)*

you have flexibility limitations—in the hip, trunk, or shoulder region. Reverse this side bend and repeat on the opposite side. Record where your flexibility limitations are.

	Right				Left	
yes		no	Hip	yes		no
yes		no	Trunk	yes		no
yes		no	Shoulder	yes		no

Hip on trunk—Stand in a golf stance and fold your arms in front of your chest. Your partner stands behind you and places his or her hands on your hips. Rotate to the side with your upper body while your partner holds your hips and evaluates your shoulder turn independently of hip turn. If you are able to rotate your upper body without moving from your hips, your weight is shifting and loading correctly. If you rotate to the right and put all of your weight on the left side, you are setting yourself up for poor swing technique—specifically a reverse pivot.

You can also try this sitting down. Have your partner place his or her hands beneath your buttocks, palm down. Rotate from your shoulders. If you are unable to rotate without your partner feeling the weight of the right side of your body pressed onto his or her right hand, you are not shifting your weight for your best golf swing; you are setting yourself up for a reverse pivot. The motion you are trying to achieve is to rotate your body and load the right side. Repeat this on the opposite side.

yes	Right	no
yes	Left	no

Trunk on hip—This test evaluates hip or lower body rotation, independent of upper body rotation. Assume a golf stance and rotate like you would for a backswing. Once in the backswing position have your partner stabilize your upper body by placing his or her left hand on the upper front part of your left shoulder and his or her right hand on the back of your right shoulder. Once your partner has stabilized you, perform a forward swing motion using your hips and trunk and then perform your backswing.

	Right				Left	
yes		no	Motion	yes		no
yes		no	Weight shift	yes		no

continued

Driving Range Evaluation Form *(continued)*

Arm cross on trunk—Stand in a golf stance and pull your arm across the front part of your body without rotating your trunk. Keep a stable lower body and a stable upper body. Do not rotate from the trunk. As you pull your arms across your body, notice when your elbow starts to bend. If it starts to bend almost immediately, you need to recruit more flexibility from the left shoulder region (see chapter 3). If your flexibility appears to be adequate, repeat on the opposite side and continue on to the next test.

Right			**Left**	
yes	no	Motion	yes	no
yes	no	Pain	yes	no

Neck on trunk—Assume your golf stance and rotate your head to the right, keeping your upper body stable. Note the position of your chin at the end range of motion. Repeat on opposite side.

Are you able to rotate your chin so it looks directly over your right shoulder? If you are unable to rotate your head completely to either direction, you are probably substituting another muscle group during your swing. This may occur during the backswing, in which you have to come off the ball to gain motion, or during the downswing, in which you have to pick up your head to keep your eye on the ball due to mobility insufficiencies in the shoulder girdle and neck.

Full rotation	**Right**	Partial rotation
Full rotation	**Left**	Partial rotation

If you experienced flexibility and rotation limitations, emphasize incorporating the drills and exercises from chapters 3, 4, 5, and 6 into your complete conditioning program.

© 1997 CDM Medical, Inc.

THE NEXT STEP

Remember that the main purpose of the self-evaluation package is to identify deficiencies in your musculoskeletal system that could affect both golf performance and injury potential. Of course, the next step is to apply the test results to a properly designed and progressive physical conditioning program. Once you are reasonably fit, you can better assess your driving abilities and limitations using the driving range evaluation form.

CHAPTER 3

FLEXIBILITY FOR FULL SWING MECHANICS

Tiger Woods is a tremendous physical talent. Woods's flexibility and strength have helped make him one of the brightest young golfers to be on the PGA Tour in a long time. Perhaps his most obvious physical gift is his extreme mobility. The range of motion and rotational speed he is able to achieve during his swing are amazing. Unlike most other touring pros, Tiger has conditioned his body to the special requirements of professional golf since an early age. He has molded his soft tissue structure to no other sport but golf; many of his competitors conditioned their bodies differently by playing various sports while growing up. Genetics is partly responsible for Tiger's exceptional framework, but his work ethic and commitment to physical conditioning have certainly enhanced his natural abilities.

When Woods's swing becomes erratic, however, it demonstrates that exceptional flexibility also can be a liability. In fact, he has said on occasion that whenever he feels that he is not swinging well, he shortens up his swing for more control.

Tiger Woods, 1997 Masters Champion and world's #2-ranked player.

Although flexibility is important, controlling the amount of flexibility that's available to you is even more important. Swinging within the limitations of your body may be the most important advice you can ever take. While flexibility is essential, it can be a liability if not used to your advantage in proper swing mechanics.

Flexibility is defined as one's available range of motion about a specific joint. The range of motion can be limited by factors such as nervous system voluntary and reflex control, muscle constraints, joint constraints, or skin and subcutaneous tissue. Flexibility might be one of the most important components of the successful golf swing because it increases the movement distance for force application. Studies have demonstrated that greater amounts of force can be produced when a muscle is prestretched before performing the activity demanded of it. When a muscle is prestretched, it creates elastic recoil that applies additional force for a more powerful contraction. This procedure is known as *preloading* the muscle.

Golf is a power sport. The golfer must be able to generate near-maximum power a certain number of times through the round. Regardless of a player's talent level, however, the most effective and powerful swings are produced when the force-generating muscles are preloaded first. We must remember that during the golf swing the preloading can take place on the downswing just as easily as it can take place on the backswing. By using segmental sequencing, good golfers will start the swinging motion with their hips and allow the trunk to lag behind slightly. As the hips initiate a forward movement, the lagging trunk muscles are stretched during the downswing. In fact, this prestretching action is even more important than the stretching that occurs during the coiling phase of the swing.

MOBILITY VERSUS STABILITY

The most important aspect of any functional movement is the principle of being in balance. Balance, as we think of it in the golfing world, is the fine line that exists between mobility and stability in your stance and swing. If you have too much flexibility, or flexibility that you are unable to control during the functional part of the golf swing, it no longer works as an asset. On the opposite side, if you are tight-jointed and stable but don't have enough mobility to produce a functional golf swing, you are unable to preload the muscle, resulting in lack of power. That is why the golf swing requires a good balance between mobility and stability. According to Gray Cook, an orthopedic physical therapy specialist, "Stability is the active muscular control exerted on a joint to redirect force and controlled movement in the presence of normal muscular flexibility and joint mobility."

Many questions regarding the effectiveness of stretching in creating this balance between mobility and stability present themselves. How long should the stretch be held? How long does it take to achieve an increase in flexibility? What is the residual effect of increased flexibility after you have stopped stretching? Other questions concern how frequently to stretch and the most effective time to stretch. The answers to all these questions have a component of individual preference. You'll attain the best results, however, by using a combination of different flexibility activities. This will ensure more comprehensive flexibility and reduce the boredom factor so that stretching will not be the most neglected fitness component in your exercise regime.

In recent years specialized flexibility equipment has been developed. A study of 40 golfers compared changes in joint flexibility and club head speed when stretching statically and when using specifically designed flexibility equipment. Several stretching devices are on the market that allow athletes to passively place and hold the body in a stretching position; the BackSystem3, Precor Stretch Trainer, StretchMate, and Prostretch are just a few. The static stretching group improved their relative flexibility and increased their club head speed by 120 percent. The group that used specialized stretching equipment did not improve their relative flexibility but increased their club head speed by 170 percent.

From this study we conclude that being stabilized at the hips on the specialized stretching equipment (as pictured below) may decrease muscle stiffness, as opposed to increasing relative flexibility. This finding has important implications with respect to power production. Improvements in general flexibility apparently might not be as useful as specifically stretching the part of the muscle chain that is tightest. This result also indicates that it might be necessary to swing within the

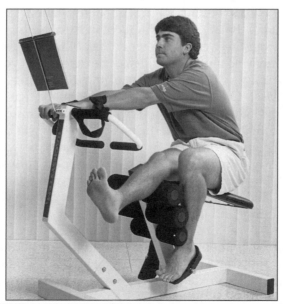

The BackSystem3 stretching device.

functional framework of your body. The piece of stretching equipment called the BackSystem3 was used in the study. Although specialized stretching equipment may make stretching more enjoyable, you should practice the basic flexibility principles even when equipment is not available.

GOLF STRETCHING ROUTINE

Stretching techniques can range from ballistic or dynamic range of motion to static stretching, active isolated stretching, or proprioceptive neuromuscular facilitation (PNF) techniques, just to name a few. Don't let the long names intimidate you, because we recommend beginning with some simple static stretches and gradually progressing to more golf-specific flexibility exercises.

Let's begin with some basic recommendations for safely improving your joint flexibility:

- Know your anatomy and its limitations.
- Learn proper stretching techniques (as provided in this chapter).
- Warm up to increase your body's temperature before stretching. Stretching after activity is more effective because the muscles are warm. Stretching also enhances the relaxing effect of the cool-down.
- A simple way to stretch is do an easy stretch for 10 seconds and an additional developmental stretch for 10 seconds.
- If possible, stretch with a partner to avoid boredom. This permits both encouragement and supervision of your technique.
- Stretch when you feel that you have to stretch. This can be done in between strengthening exercises or during your golf game.

Before playing or stretching, do an adequate warm-up activity to raise your body temperature. Preceding your stretches with a brisk walk or other appropriate aerobic exercise, such as stationary cycling or stepping, makes your muscles more responsive and resistant to injury. Five to 15 minutes of warm-up exercise increases muscle extensibility and lets you stretch more safely and effectively.

To achieve the best stretch possible, make certain either the near or far body segment is in a fixed position. If this does not occur, the result will be two moving parts and a stretch possibly occurring where it should not occur. When you perform your flexibility exercises, be sure to stretch only one muscle group at a time.

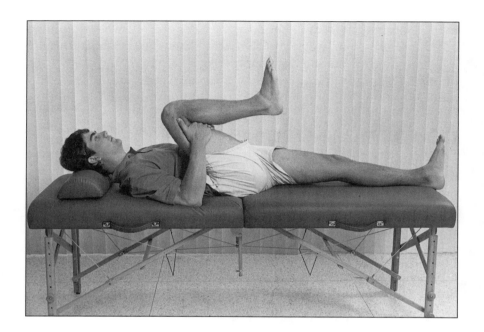

KNEE TO CHEST

Focus: Lower back and gluteal muscles

Procedure:

1. Lie on your back with your neck supported and body extended.
2. Flex one knee and slide your foot toward your buttocks.
3. Grasp with both hands behind the flexed knee.
4. Pull your knee toward your chest.
5. Hold the stretch and relax.
6. Exhale and re-extend your leg slowly to prevent possible pain or spasm; repeat with other leg.

Duration: Hold for 20 seconds or 2 × 10 to 12 seconds.

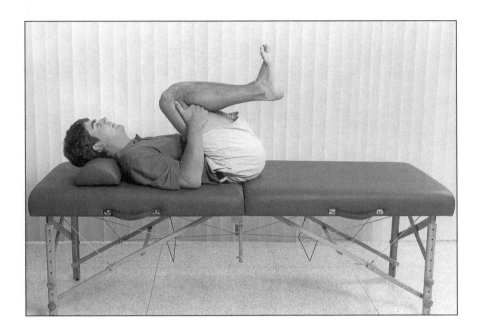

DOUBLE KNEES TO CHEST

Focus: Lower back

Procedure:

1. Lie on your back with your neck supported and body extended.

2. Flex your knees and slide your feet toward your buttocks.

3. Grasp behind your thighs to prevent hyperflexion (too much bending) of the knees.

4. Exhale, pull your knees toward your chest and shoulders, and elevate your hips off the floor.

5. Hold the stretch and relax.

6. Exhale and re-extend your legs slowly one at a time to prevent possible pain or spasm.

Duration: Hold for 20 seconds or 2 × 10 to 12 seconds.

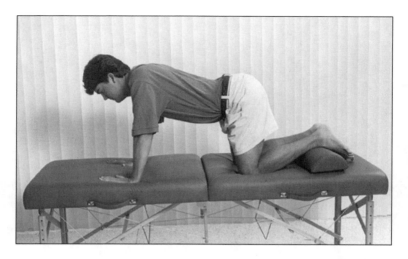

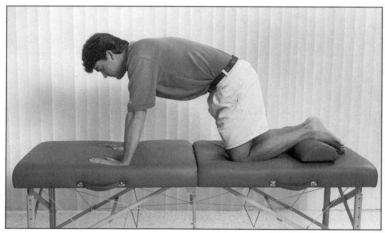

CAT AND CAMEL

Focus: Upper back

Procedure:

1. Kneel on all fours.
2. Extend your arms forward and lower your chest toward the floor.
3. Exhale, extend your shoulders, and press down on the floor with your arms to produce an arch in your back.
4. Hold the stretch and relax.

Duration: Hold for 20 seconds or 2 × 10 to 12 seconds.

HAMSTRING

Focus: Hamstrings

Procedure:

1. Lie flat on your back with legs extended.
2. Raise one leg and grasp your thigh with both hands, while keeping the knee extended and your other leg flat. To increase the stretch, pull the leg toward your chest.
3. Hold the stretch and relax.
4. Exhale while you slowly release the stretch and repeat with the other leg.

Duration: Hold for 20 seconds or 2 × 10 to 12 seconds.

Tips:

- You can also position yourself in a doorway and use the door frame to hold your elevated leg. The closer you move your buttocks toward the door frame, the more intense the stretch.
- To intensify the stretch, use a folded towel wrapped around the foot of the raised leg. By pulling on the towel, the leg can be pulled away from the doorframe and closer to your chest.

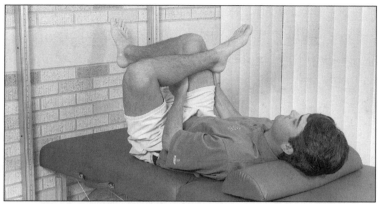

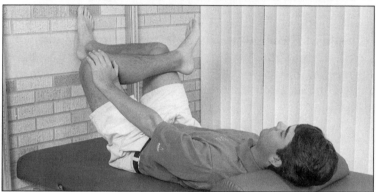

FIGURE FOUR

Focus: Hips and gluteal muscles

Procedure:

1. Lie on your back with both feet resting on the wall or a door. Use a towel or neck rest to support your neck.

2. Bend your knees and hips to a 90-degree angle.

3. Cross your left foot and rest it on your right knee.

4. Use your left hand and push your left knee away from your chest until you feel a gentle stretch in your hips or buttocks region.

5. Return to starting position. Repeat with the other leg

Duration: Hold for 20 seconds or 2 × 10 to 12 seconds.

Tip: If you do not feel the stretch, place both hands under your right knee and slowly pull your right leg toward your chest until you feel a stretch in your buttocks.

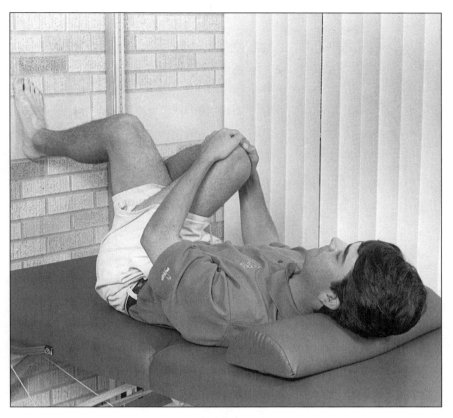

CROSSOVER

Focus: Hips and gluteal muscles

Procedure:

1. Lie on your back with your head supported by a rolled-up towel.

2. Place both feet flat on a wall, with your hips and knees bent to 90 degrees.

3. Cross your left leg over your right thigh.

4. Place your right hand on your left thigh and pull it slowly toward the floor, until you feel a stretch on the outside of your left hip.

Duration: Hold for 20 seconds each leg.

Tip: Stop if you feel pinching in the groin region.

KNEELING HIP FLEXOR

Focus: Hip flexors and upper thigh

Procedure:

1. Stand upright with the legs straddled (spread sideways) about two feet apart.

2. Flex one knee, lower your body, and place the opposite knee on the surface.

3. Roll the back foot under so that the top of the instep rests on the surface.

4. Place your hands on your hips (some people may prefer placing one hand on the forward knee and one hand at your side) and keep the front knee bent at 90 degrees as much as possible.

5. Exhale and slowly push the front of the hip of the back leg toward the floor.

6. Hold the stretch and relax.

Duration: Hold for 20 seconds or 2 × 10 to 12 seconds.

QUAD STRETCH

Focus: Middle and upper quadriceps

Procedure:

1. Stand holding onto a bar or table for support with your right hand.
2. Exhale as you slowly lift your left leg off the ground and grasp the left foot with your left hand.
3. Inhale, and slowly pull your heel toward your buttocks.
4. Hold the stretch and relax. Repeat with the other leg.

Duration: Hold for 20 seconds or 2 × 10 to 12 seconds.

Tip: This exercise can be an intense stretch. To protect your lower back, stand straight and contract the abdominal muscles.

PEC STRETCH

Focus: Upper chest (*pectoralis* muscles)

Procedure:

1. Stand upright facing a corner or open doorway.
2. Raise your elbows to shoulder height at your sides, bend your elbows so that your forearms point straight up, and place your palms against the walls or doorframe to stretch the sternal section of the *pectoralis* muscles on both sides.
3. Exhale and lean your entire body forward.
4. Hold the stretch and relax.

Duration: Hold for 20 seconds or 2 × 10 to 12 seconds.

INVERTED HURDLER'S STRETCH

Focus: Hamstrings

Procedure:

1. Sit upright on the floor with both legs straight and about 90 degrees apart.
2. Flex one knee and slide the heel until it touches the inner side of the opposite thigh.
3. Lower the outer side of the thigh and calf of the bent leg onto the floor.
4. Exhale and, while keeping the extended leg straight, bend at the hip and lower your extended upper torso onto the extended thigh.
5. Hold the stretch and relax.

Duration: Hold for 20 seconds or 2 × 10 to 12 seconds.

CALF STRETCH

Focus: *Gastrocnemius* muscle and Achilles tendon

Procedure:

1. Stand upright facing a wall; stand slightly more than arm's length from the wall.
2. Bend your right leg forward while keeping your left leg straight.
3. Lean into the wall keeping back straight and bending elbows.
4. Exhale and hold stretch; repeat with other leg.

Duration: Hold for 20 seconds or 2 × 10 to 12 seconds.

Tip: To feel the stretch closer to the heel, bend the rear leg (at the knee) while keeping the foot on the ground.

Stretching for Young Golfers

Youth sports, including golf, have increased in both numbers and popularity. With the appearance of new, young talent in the PGA, LPGA, and Nike tours, children are starting to view golf as being very cool. Because children have not completed their physical maturation, an injury at this time could result in permanent developmental disability and lead to long-term functional problems. One of the ways to reduce injury risk for young golfers is to have them warm up and stretch before play. These same preventive procedures also should enhance their performance ability.

Because the trunk serves as the link between the upper and lower bodies, it must be strong enough to transfer forces between these segments. The child is at greatest risk for injury during a growth spurt, which is when large increases in height are observed. During this stage, the child has a tendency to develop tight low back, hamstring, and hip musculature in combination with weak abdominal muscles and a swayback posture. This can lead to compensatory maneuvers and increased injury risk. Problems can range from common strains and sprains, to fractures, disc injuries, vertebral wedging, stress reactions, vertebral slippage, and overuse injuries.

Make training modifications for any golfers under 20, especially those undergoing the added vulnerability of a growth spurt. Rehabilitation and prevention programs can range from strengthening and stretching exercises to immobilization and, in some instances, rest. Remembering that the muscles might not grow as fast as the bone, flexibility becomes imperative during this critical developmental period.

ON-COURSE WARM-UP

Perform your on-course warm-up using the following flexibility exercises. These exercises can be done even while in your golf cart. If you are running late to the practice tee, be sure to at least do the following stretches: seated hamstring, seated club lat stretch, seated low back and groin, pec neck, standing hip flexor, bow bend, body rotation, and abdominal hollow.

SEATED LOW BACK AND GROIN

Focus: Lower back and groin

Procedure:

1. Sit upright in a cart (or chair) with your legs separated slightly.

2. Exhale, extend your upper torso, bend at the hip, and slowly lower your stomach between your thighs.

3. Hold the stretch.

Duration: Hold for 20 seconds or 2 × 10 to 12 seconds.

Tip: Be sure to exhale as you bend at the hip.

SEATED HAMSTRING

Focus: Hamstrings

Procedure:

1. Sit in a cart (or chair) with your feet approximately shoulder-width apart. Assume a position to allow a little bit of arch in the lower back region.

2. While maintaining the arched-back position, attempt to straighten one of your legs.

3. Perform the movement slowly, maintaining the slight arch throughout the whole exercise.

4. End with one knee more extended while maintaining an arched-back posture.

5. Do all repetitions on one side and then the other.

Duration: Hold for 20 seconds or 2×10 to 12 seconds.

SEATED FIGURE FOUR

Focus: Hips and gluteal muscles

Procedure:

1. Sit up straight in a cart or on a chair with both feet flat on the floor.
2. Lift your right foot and rest it on your left knee.
3. Place both hands on your right leg and push your knee away from your chest until you feel a gentle stretch in your hips or buttocks region.
4. Hold the stretch, relax, and repeat with left leg.

Duration: Hold for 20 seconds.

SEATED CROSSOVER

Focus: Hips and gluteal muscles

Procedure:

1. Sit up straight in a cart or on a chair with both feet flat on the floor.
2. Lift your right leg and cross it over your left thigh.
3. Place both hands on your right leg and pull your right leg toward the left side of your body until you feel a gentle stretch in your hips.
4. Hold the stretch, relax, and repeat with left leg.

Duration: Hold for 20 seconds.

Tip: Stop if you feel pinching in the groin region.

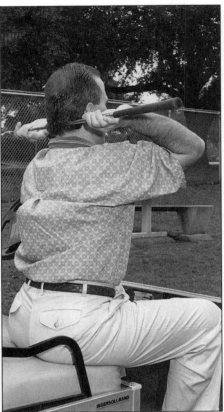

SEATED CLUB LAT

Focus: Upper back

Procedure:

1. Sit in a chair or in your cart with your feet resting flat on the floor and your back slightly arched.

2. Grasp the bar of the club with both hands and position it behind your head at ear level (just below the base of the skull). Make sure your hands are directly above your elbows.

3. Rotate your elbows upward (toward the ceiling or the sky), holding the position for three counts.

4. Return the elbows to the neutral position.

Duration: Hold for 15 seconds or 5 × 3 seconds.

Tip: Make sure your hands are directly above your elbows.

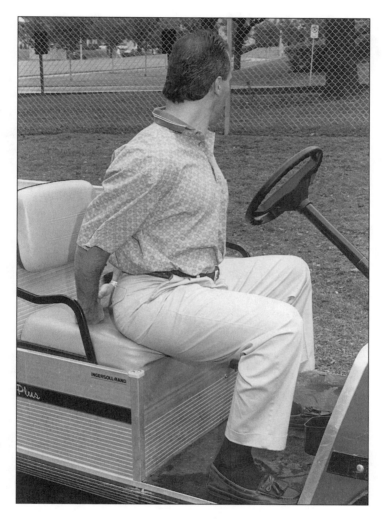

PEC NECK

Focus: Neck and upper pectoralis major

Procedure:

1. Stand or sit with your shoulder blades pulled down and back, as if you were squeezing something between them.

2. While keeping your shoulder blades down and backward, rotate your head to the left and hold.

3. Repeat on opposite side.

Duration: Hold for 20 seconds or 2 × 10 to 12 seconds.

STANDING HIP FLEXOR

Focus: Quadriceps and hip flexors

Procedure:

1. In a standing position, place one foot on an elevated surface.

2. Roll the pelvis forward (pulling your buttocks in).

3. Place your opposite leg behind you. Keep the foot pointed straight ahead.

4. While keeping your back straight, lunge forward so that a stretch is felt in the front part of the thigh of the rear leg. Repeat on the other side.

Duration: Hold for 20 seconds or 2 × 10 to 12 seconds.

STANDING ROTATOR CUFF

Focus: Shoulders and upper back muscles

Procedure:

1. Stand in upright position with feet in split stance
2. Hold club in right arm with elbow bent and rotate arm back.
3. Reach under with left arm and grab club to support elbow.

Duration: Hold for 20 seconds or 2 × 10 to 12 seconds.

BOW BEND

Focus: Outer hips, sides, and shoulder muscles

Procedure:

1. Stand in an upright position with the arms elevated over the head and holding a club beyond shoulder-width apart.

2. Place the right leg behind the left leg and try to keep the toes pointed straight ahead.

3. Allow the right hip to fall or press out to the right. Bend to the left.

4. Use your left arm to pull your right arm down, close to the head.

5. Repeat on the opposite side by placing the left foot behind the right foot and following the same sequence.

Duration: Hold for 20 seconds or 2 × 10 to 12 seconds.

Tip: The stretch should be done in this sequence so that the stretch is felt first in the outer hip, followed by the side, ending with the shoulder region.

SEATED SPINAL TWIST

Focus: Hips, abdominal and gluteal muscles

Procedure:

1. Sit up straight in your cart with both feet on the floor.
2. Keeping feet on the floor, rotate your legs to one side and your upper body to the other side.
3. Exhale and rotate as far as you can by holding onto the seat.

Duration: Hold for 20 seconds or 2 × 10 to 12 seconds.

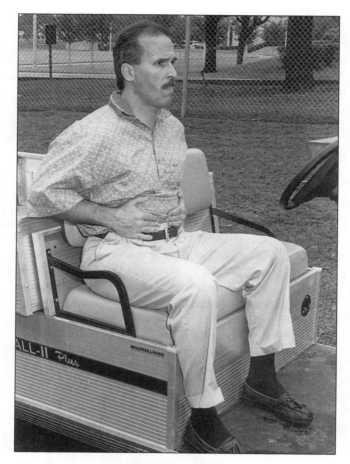

ABDOMINAL HOLLOW

Focus: To promote trunk stability and activate the abdominal and small muscles

Procedure:

1. Sit in the cart with your back straight, knees bent, and feet resting firmly on the floor.
2. Pull your tummy in and up under your rib cage.
3. Hold for duration of stretch and relax.

Duration: Hold 20 seconds or 10 × 2 seconds.

Tip: Perform the exercise so that neither the pelvis nor the spine move, but remain stable while doing this type of deep abdominal muscle contraction.

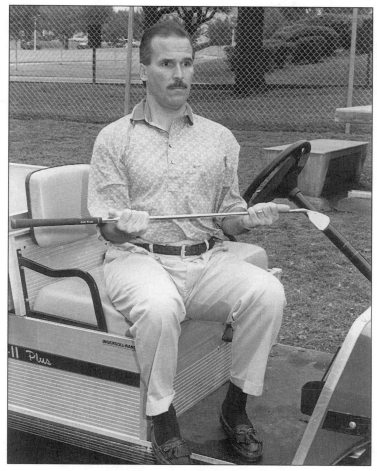

ROTATOR CUFF ISOMETRICS

Focus: Rotator cuffs and scapula stabilizers

Procedure:

1. Hold a club or stick in both hands with arms against your side and palms facing upward.

2. Attempt to pull hands apart while still holding the club tightly (outward).

3. Now attempt to push hands together while holding the club tightly (inward).

Duration: Hold for 10 seconds or 6 × 2 to 3 seconds.

Tip: Maintain an erect posture to achieve optimal external rotation.

THE NEXT STEP

Flexibility plays a major role in developing optimal swing mechanics. If you have tight joints or stiff muscles, you cannot properly preload muscle actions for powerful and functional swing movements. Flexibility must be balanced with stability to attain best results and high levels of golf performance. We discuss how to achieve this stability with the strength training exercises in the next chapter.

CHAPTER 4

STRENGTH FOR MAXIMUM DISTANCE AND CONTROL

As a collegiate golfer at Georgia Tech,

David Duval was so talented that he competed successfully despite having a less-than-high physical fitness level. Although his coach, Puggy Blackman, established and encouraged a conditioning program, David did not make physical training a priority.

Since that time David has emerged as one of the bright young talents on the PGA Tour. Before undertaking a stringent weight reduction and strength training program, David scored well but never won. This has all changed: David has won several tour events after dedicating himself to purposeful exercise, proper nutrition, and good discipline in off-the-course activities. Although this evidence is anecdotal, to David and those who have watched his career closely, it seems clear that a solid strength and conditioning program has taken him from being a very good player to the great player that he is today.

© Action Images

David Duval began an intensive training program prior to becoming the world's #1-ranked player.

STRONGER MUSCLES FOR BETTER GOLF

Generally speaking, golf is a slow-pace sport very different from fast-movement activities such as basketball, tennis, aerobic dance, or skiing. The exception to this rule is the explosive action of the golf swing, which places significant stress on shoulder, elbow, and wrist joints, and produces high torque forces on the low back and hip structures. Consequently, if you are not strong and fit in these parts, you could experience game-limiting injuries in these and other areas of the body.

Although you could increase your hitting power and reduce your injury risk by practicing proper swing mechanics under the watchful eye of a professional golf instructor, you also could improve your swing and decrease your potential for injury by performing appropriate stretching and strengthening exercises that produce a flexible and strong musculoskeletal system. As you achieve higher levels of fitness, you can generate more power with less effort, thereby producing a smoother swing with greater club head speed. You will develop more force without forcing the action, which is essential for long and consistent drives.

Why? Your muscles have the ability to relax and lengthen. Well-designed stretching exercises enhance your muscles' lengthening capacity, thereby increasing your movement range and improving your joint flexibility. Your muscles also have the ability to contract and shorten, producing varying levels of movement force in the process. Progressive strength training enhances your muscles' contraction capacity, thereby increasing your movement force and improving your musculoskeletal function. Such conditioning provides the dual benefit of more power production and greater resistance to potentially damaging forces.

By doing a basic program of stretching and strengthening exercises, you can simultaneously produce driving power more easily and absorb swing forces more safely. Because these are the keys to successful and enduring golf participation, you should carefully consider starting a sensible golf conditioning program.

As has been mentioned in preceding chapters, the golf swing is one of the most complex and unnatural actions in all athletic activities. In fact, you probably spend many hours at the driving range to develop more effective swing mechanics. Some of your practice time may be better spent doing appropriate golf conditioning exercises, however, to develop the physical ability necessary to swing the way you should.

Several research studies have looked at the effects of basic conditioning programs for golfers. The golfers in these studies spent just 25 to 35 minutes a day, three times per week, in the fitness center. All did 12 to 14 strength exercises on Nautilus machines and some also performed six stretches on a StretchMate apparatus. Table 4.1 presents the basic strength training exercises, the major muscle groups they address, their relevance to the golf swing, and home training alternatives using free weights. If you are new to strength training, it might be best to begin with machine exercises because they may be easier to learn and perform properly. Free-weight exercises offer greater versatility and require more movement control, however, which might be advantageous for some golfers. For most practical purposes, a combination of machine and free-weight exercises should provide a successful and satisfying strength training program.

Table 4.1   Basic Strength Training Exercises for Overall Muscle Conditioning

Nautilus exercise	Muscles addressed	Effect on golf swing	Dumbbell exercise
Leg extension	Quadriceps	Power production	Step-up
Leg curl	Hamstrings	Power production	Lunge
Leg press	Quadriceps, hamstrings, and gluteal muscles	Power production	Squat
Low back	Erector spinae	Force transfer— lower to upper body	Back extension (bodyweight)
Abdominal curl	Rectus abdominis	Force transfer— lower to upper body	Trunk curl (bodyweight)
Rotary torso	Internal obliques External obliques	Force transfer— lower to upper body	Trunk curl/twist (bodyweight)
Chest crossover	Pectoralis major	Swing action	Bench press
Super pullover	Latissimus dorsi	Swing action	One-arm bent row
Lateral raise	Deltoids	Swing action	Lateral raise
Biceps curl	Biceps	Club control	Standing curl
Triceps extension	Triceps	Club control	Overhead triceps extension
Super forearm flexion	Forearm flexors	Club control	Wrist curl
Super forearm extension	Forearm extensors	Club control	Wrist extension

Table 4.2   Changes Experienced by Golfers Following Eight Weeks of
Training

Factors	Strength training only (N = 52)	Strength training and stretching (N = 25)	All participants (N = 77)
Club head speed (mph)	+2.6	+5.2	+3.4
Body weight (lb)	–0.7	+1.0	–0.2
Percent fat	–2.3	–1.7	–2.0
Fat weight (lb)	–4.6	–3.0	–4.1
Lean (muscle) weight (lb)	+3.9	+4.0	+3.9
Mean blood pressure (mmHg)	–4.4	–4.8	–4.5
Muscle strength (lb)	+56	+56	+56

After eight weeks of strength training, the golfers in these studies made significant improvements in their driving power, as indicated by faster club head speeds. As shown in table 4.2, the golfers also replaced four pounds of fat with four pounds of muscle, increased their muscle strength by almost 60 percent, and reduced their resting blood pressure by more than 4 mmHg. Even more impressive, the golfers who also strength trained and did stretching exercises experienced twice as much increase in club head speed as well as a 30 percent improvement in overall joint flexibility.

These results should be compelling for golfers who want to play better, look better, feel better, and avoid injuries. It is encouraging to note that all the golfers who completed the strength training program remained injury-free throughout the entire golf season. Furthermore, most reported a higher overall level of play, with less fatigue and more energy than they had experienced in many years. Clearly, sensible strength training is beneficial for both the golfer and the game.

The basic program of strength exercise is simple, short, and easy to complete. We recommend that golfers do one set each of 13 exercises, for a total of just 13 training sets per session. Use a resistance that permits between 8 and 12 repetitions performed at a controlled speed through a full movement range. When 12 repetitions are completed in good form, increase the weight load by 5 percent or less. The entire strength workout should take about 25 minutes, three days a week. The latest studies have

Table 4.3 Sample Workout Card for Machine and Dumbbell Exercises

Name:

Machine exercise	Seat setting	Workout							
Leg extension		Weight / Reps							
Leg curl		Weight / Reps							
Leg press		Weight / Reps							
Low back		Weight / Reps							
Abdominal curl		Weight / Reps							
Rotary torso		Weight / Reps							
Chest crossover		Weight / Reps							
Super pullover		Weight / Reps							
Lateral raise		Weight / Reps							
Biceps curl		Weight / Reps							
Triceps extension		Weight / Reps							
Forearm flexion		Weight / Reps							
Forearm extension		Weight / Reps							

Dumbbell exercise	Seat setting	Workout							
Step up		Weight / Reps							
Lunge		Weight / Reps							
Squat		Weight / Reps							
Back extension (bodyweight)		Weight / Reps							
Trunk curl (bodyweight)		Weight / Reps							
Trunk curl twist (bodyweight)		Weight / Reps							
Bench press		Weight / Reps							
One-arm bent row		Weight / Reps							
Lateral raise		Weight / Reps							
Standing curl		Weight / Reps							
Overhead triceps extension		Weight / Reps							
Wrist curl		Weight / Reps							
Wrist extension		Weight / Reps							

shown about 90 percent of the benefit can be realized from only two strength training sessions per week, however, which is good news for time-pressured people and active golfers.

With these facts in mind, here are your basic guidelines for a beginning strength training program:

- Perform one exercise for each major muscle group for overall and balanced muscle conditioning.
- Perform one set of each exercise.
- Use a resistance that lets you complete between 8 and 12 repetitions.
- Increase the resistance by 5 percent or less upon reaching 12 good repetitions.
- Perform every repetition at a controlled speed, typically two seconds for the lifting phase and four seconds for the lowering phase.
- Perform every repetition through a full range of joint movement (as long as you do not experience discomfort in doing so).
- Strength-train two or three nonconsecutive days per week.
- Keep a record of each workout to monitor your training progress as indicated on the sample workout card (table 4.3).

Generally speaking, this program should produce noticeable changes in your muscle strength and body composition within one month. After two months of training, you should be about 50 to 60 percent stronger on your exercise weight loads. You should also replace up to four pounds of fat with four pounds of muscle, which should help you look, feel, and function much better than before you started training. Your fat/muscle changes can be assessed best by body composition tests, typically performed with skinfold calipers. You also should notice firmer muscles in your legs, arms, and upper body, in addition to more slack in your waistband.

We recommend that your strength training program become a standard component of your lifestyle. Even when you achieve a high level of muscle conditioning, regular strength training is necessary to maintain your physical capacity and performance ability.

RECOMMENDED MACHINE EXERCISES

LEG EXTENSION

Focus: Quadriceps

Beginning Position:

1. Adjust the seat so your knees are in line with machine's axis of rotation (where machine pivots), typically indicated by a red dot.

2. Sit with your back firmly against the seat pad.

3. Position ankles behind the roller pad, knees flexed about 90 degrees.

4. Grip handles.

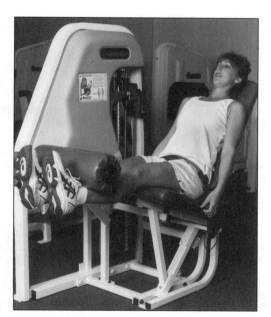

Upward Movement Phase:

1. Push the roller pad slowly upward until your knees are extended.

2. Exhale throughout the upward movement.

Downward Movement Phase:

1. Return the roller pad slowly to the starting position.

2. Inhale throughout the lowering movement.

Tips and Modifications:

- Knee pain, particularly in positions of knee flexion: Double-pin the weight stack or use the built-in range limiter to restrict action to the pain-free range of movement.

- Inability to reach full knee extension: Use lighter weight load to permit greater movement range.

LEG CURL

Focus: Hamstrings

Beginning Position:

1. Adjust the seat so your knee joint is in line with machine's axis of rotation, typically indicated by a red dot.
2. Sit with your back firmly against the seat pad.
3. Position your lower legs between the roller pads, knees extended.
4. Grip handles.

Backward Movement Phase:

1. Pull the roller pads slowly backward until your knees are fully flexed.
2. Exhale throughout the pulling movement.

Forward Movement Phase:

1. Return the roller pads slowly to the starting position.
2. Inhale throughout the return movement.

Tips and Modifications:

- Inability to reach full knee flexion: Use lighter weight load to permit greater movement range.

- Discomfort in low back positions of knee flexion: Contract abdominal muscles to maintain flat back contact with seatback.

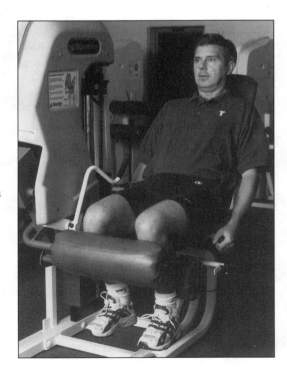

LEG PRESS

Focus: Quadriceps, hamstrings, gluteal muscles

Beginning Position:

1. Adjust the seat so your knees are flexed to 90 degrees or less.
2. Sit with your back firmly against the seat pad.
3. Place your feet flat on the foot pad, in line with knees and hips.
4. Grip the handles.

Forward Movement Phase:

1. Push the foot pad forward slowly until your knees are almost extended, but not locked.
2. Keep the feet, knees, and hips aligned.
3. Exhale throughout the pushing phase.

Backward Movement Phase:

1. Return the foot pad slowly to the starting position.
2. Inhale throughout the return movement.

Tips and Modifications:

- Knee pain in various positions of knee extension: Keep the knees directly behind the feet and the same width as your hips. Do not flex knees beyond 90 degrees in rear position, and stop short of lockout in the forward position.

- Hip or groin pain in positions of hip flexion: Limit hip flexion to pain-free range of movement, usually consistent with 90 degrees of knee flexion.

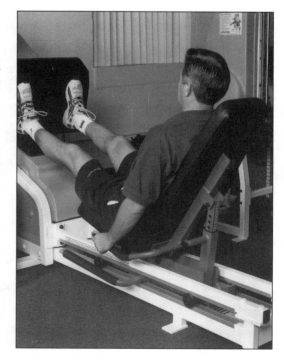

LOW BACK

Focus: Erector spinae

Beginning Position:

1. Sit all the way back on the seat and adjust the foot pad so that your knees are slightly higher than your hips.

2. Secure seat belt across thighs and hips.

3. Cross your arms across the chest.

4. Place your upper back firmly against the pad with the trunk flexed forward.

Backward Movement Phase:

1. Push the upper back against the pad until your trunk is fully extended.

2. Keep your head in line with the torso.

3. Exhale throughout the extension movement.

Forward Movement Phase:

1. Return the pad slowly to the starting position.

2. Inhale throughout the return movement.

Tips and Modifications:

- Discomfort in the low back area: Abbreviate trunk extension to a pain-free range of move- ment.

- Strain in the neck area: Maintain neutral head position through- out exercise.

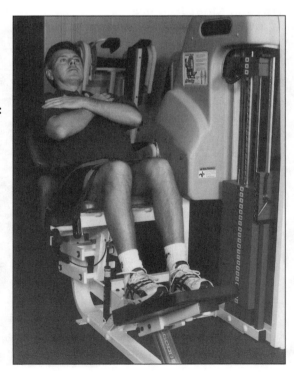

ABDOMINAL CURL

Focus: Rectus abdominis

Beginning Position:

1. Adjust the seat so your navel is aligned with the machine's axis of rotation, typically indicated by a red dot.
2. Sit with your upper back firmly against the pad.
3. Place your elbows on the arm pads and your hands on the handles.

Forward Movement Phase:

1. Pull the pad forward slowly until the trunk is fully flexed by contracting the abdominal muscles (as tight as you can get them).
2. Keep your upper back firmly against the pad.
3. Exhale throughout the forward movement.

Backward Movement Phase:

1. Return the pad slow-ly to the starting position.
2. Inhale throughout the return movement.

Tips and Modifications:

- Discomfort in the low back area: Abbreviate trunk flexion to a pain-free range of movement.

- Strain in the neck area: Maintain a neutral head position throughout the exercise.

ROTARY TORSO

Focus: External obliques, internal obliques

Beginning Position

1.   Sit all the way back on the seat with the torso erect, facing forward.
2.   Wrap your legs around the seat extension.
3.   Position your upper arms against the arm pads.

Left Movement Phase:

1.   Turn the torso slowly left, about 45 degrees.
2.   Exhale throughout the rotation.

Return Movement Phase:

1.   Return the torso slowly to the starting position (facing forward).
2.   Inhale throughout the return movement.
3.   Change the seat position and repeat the exercise to the right.

Tips and Modifications:

- Discomfort in shoulders, midsection, or hips: Reduce the torso turning distance to a pain-free range of movement.
- Pressure in arms: Place equal emphasis on both arms by repositioning so that one arm pulls and one arm pushes the arm pads.

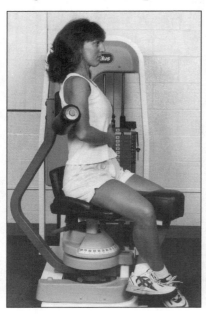 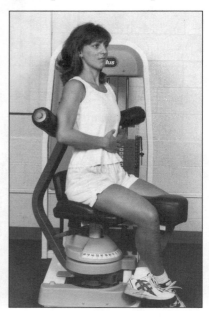

CHEST CROSSOVER

Focus: Pectoralis major

Beginning Position:

1. Adjust the seat so your shoulders are in line with the machine's axes of rotation (typically indicated by red dots) and your upper arms are parallel to the floor.
2. Sit with head, shoulders, and back firmly against the seat pad.
3. Position your forearms against the arm pads and your hands on the handles.

Forward Movement Phase:

1. Pull the arm pads slowly together, using arms more than hands.
2. Keep your wrists straight.
3. Exhale throughout the pulling movement.

Backward Movement Phase:

1. Return the arm pads slowly to the starting position.
2. Inhale throughout the return movement.

Tips and Modifications:

- Pain in shoulders or strain in chest area: Reduce backward movement range so that your hands are always in front of your shoulders.
- Discomfort in elbow area: Reposition the seat or add a back pad so that the movement pads make greater contact with your arms.

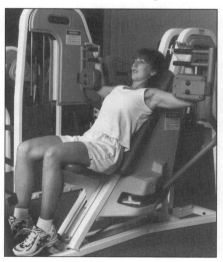 

SUPER PULLOVER

Focus: Latissimus dorsi

Beginning Position:

1. Adjust the seat so your shoulders are in line with the machine's axis of rotation, typically indicated by a red dot.

2. Sit with your back firmly against the seat pad, seat belt secured.

3. Place your feet on the foot lever and press forward to bring the arm pads into a starting position near your face.

4. Position your arms against the arm pads and your hands on the bar.

5. Release the foot pad.

Downward Movement Phase:

1. Pull the arm pads downward slowly, using your arms more than hands, until the bar touches your body.

2. Keep your wrists straight.

3. Round your back slightly during downward movement.

4. Exhale throughout the downward movement.

Upward Movement Phase:

1. Return the arm pads slowly to the starting position.

2. Inhale throughout the return movement.

3. After completing the final repetition, place your feet on the foot lever, press forward to hold the weight stack, remove your arms, and lower the weight stack slowly.

Tips and Modifications:

- Pain in shoulders: Reduce backward movement to the pain-free range of exercise action.

- Discomfort in low back area: Contract the abdominal muscles during downward movement to flatten your back against the seatback when movement pads are below shoulder level.

MACHINE LATERAL RAISE

Focus: Deltoids

Beginning Position:

1. Adjust the seat so your shoulders are in line with the machine's axis of rotation, typically indicated by red dots.

2. Sit with your head, shoulders, and back firmly against the seat pad.

3. Position your arms against the arm pads and your hands on the handles, with your arms close to your sides.

Upward Movement Phase:

1. Lift the arm pads upward slowly, using arms more than hands.

2. Keep your wrists straight.

3. Stop the upward movement when your arms are parallel to the floor.

4. Exhale throughout the lifting movement.

Downward Movement Phase:

1. Return the pads slowly to the starting position.

2. Inhale throughout the lowering movement.

Tips and Modifications:

- Pain in shoulders: Stop upward movement before your upper arms are parallel to the floor.

- Pain in wrists: Grasp the handles lightly for stability, but do not use your hands for lifting purposes.

- Discomfort in low back area: Contract the abdominal muscles to maintain flat-back contact with the seatback.

BICEPS CURL

Focus: Biceps

Beginning Position:

1. Adjust the seat so your elbows are in line with the machine's axis of rotation, typically indicated by red dots.
2. Grasp the handles with an underhand grip, elbows slightly flexed.
3. Sit with your chest against the chest pad.

Upward Movement Phase:

1. Curl the handles upward slowly until your elbows are fully flexed.
2. Keep your wrists straight.
3. Exhale throughout the lifting movement.

Downward Movement Phase:

1. Return the handles slowly to the starting position.
2. Inhale throughout the lowering movement.

Tips and Modifications:

- Pain in elbows: Reposition your elbows in line with the machine's axis of rotation or stop about 30 degrees short of full elbow extension on lowering movements.

- Pain in wrists: Maintain a neutral wrist position throughout each repetition.

- Discomfort in the lower back area: Maintain erect posture and avoid arching your back.

TRICEPS EXTENSION

Focus: Triceps

Beginning Position:

1. Adjust the seat so your elbows are in line with the machine's axis of rotation, typically indicated by red dots.
2. Sit with your back firmly against the seat pad.
3. Place the sides of your hands against the hand pads and allow them to move close to your face.

Downward Movement Phase:

1. Push the hand pads downward slowly until your arms are fully extended.
2. Keep your wrists straight.
3. Exhale throughout the lifting movement.

Upward Movement Phase:

1. Return the pads slowly to the starting position.
2. Inhale throughout the return movement.

Tips and Modifications:

- Pain in elbows: Reposition your elbows in line with the machine's axis of rotation or stop about 30 degrees short of full elbow flexion on the upward movement phase.

- Pain in wrists: Maintain a neutral wrist position throughout each repetition.

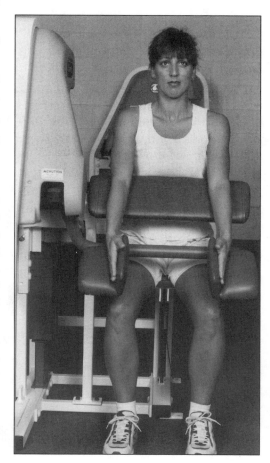

SUPER FOREARM

Focus: Wrist flexors, extensors, pronators, supinators

Beginning Position:

This machine has five separate exercises for the forearm muscles. For each exercise, adjust the seat so that the forearms rest securely and comfortably on the arm pads. Grasp the appropriate handles for the desired wrist action.

- For wrist flexion, grasp forward handles with an underhand grip.
- For wrist extension, grasp the forward handles with an overhand grip.
- For wrist pronators, grasp the rear handles with an underhand grip.
- For wrist supination, grasp the rear handles with an overhand grip.

Upward Movement Phase:

1. Move the handles in the direction that lifts the weight stack.
2. Exhale throughout the lifting action.

Downward Movement Phase:

1. Move the handles in the direction that lowers the weight stack.
2. Inhale throughout the lowering action.

Tips and Modifications:

- Discomfort in wrists or forearms: Abbreviate the lifting action to a pain-free range of movement.

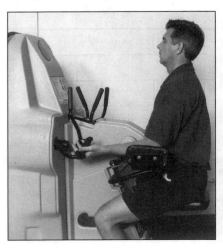 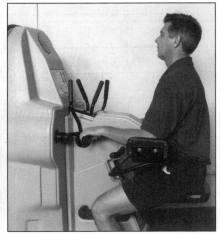

RECOMMENDED FREE-WEIGHT EXERCISES

DUMBBELL STEP-UP

Focus: Quadriceps, hamstrings, gluteal muscles

Beginning Position:

1. Grasp the dumbbells and stand erect several inches in front of a stair step, with feet hip-width apart and parallel to one another.
2. Position the dumbbells with your palms facing the outside surfaces of the thighs.

Upward Movement Phase:

1. Place your left foot on the step, followed by your right foot.
2. Exhale throughout the upward movement.

Downward Movement Phase:

1. Place your left foot on the floor, followed by the right foot, standing again in the beginning position.
2. Inhale throughout the downward movement.
3. Keep your head up, eyes fixed straight ahead, shoulders back, and your back erect throughout the upward and downward phases of this exercise.
4. Alternate stepping up with the left and right legs.

Tips and Modifications:

- Pain in the knee area: Use a smaller step or a sturdy box that does not require as much vertical movement.
- Discomfort in shoulders, arms, or hands: Hold the dumbbells on your shoulders rather than beside your hips.
- Pain in low back area: Substitute the dumbbell squat exercise.

DUMBBELL LUNGE

Focus: Quadriceps, hamstrings, gluteal muscles

Beginning Position:

1. Grasp the dumbbells and stand erect with your feet about hip-width apart and parallel to one another.
2. Position the dumbbells with your palms facing the outside surfaces of your thighs.

Downward Movement Phase:

1. Step forward far enough with your left foot that the left knee is bent about 90 degrees and is directly above your foot.
2. Inhale throughout the downward movement.

Upward Movement Phase:

1. Push off the left foot and return to the beginning position.
2. Exhale throughout the upward movement.
3. Keep your head up, eyes fixed straight ahead, shoulders back, and back erect throughout the upward and downward movement phases of this exercise.
4. Alternate stepping forward with the left and right legs.

Tips and Modifications:

- Pain or pressure in knee area: Step forward a little farther to make sure the knee is above (and never ahead of) your foot, or abbreviate the descent to permit pain-free lunge action.
- Discomfort in shoulders, arms, or hands: Hold the dumbbells on your shoulders rather than beside your hips.
- Pain in low back area: Substitute the dumbbell squat exercise.

DUMBBELL SQUAT

Focus: Quadriceps, hamstrings, gluteal muscles

Beginning Position:

1. Grasp the dumbbells and stand erect with your feet about hip-width apart and parallel to one another.

2. Position the dumbbells with your palms facing the outside surfaces of your thighs.

Downward Movement Phase:

1. Squat down slowly until your thighs are parallel to the floor.

2. Inhale throughout the downward movement.

Upward Movement Phase:

1. Move upward by slowly straightening the knees and hips.

2. Exhale throughout the upward movement.

3. Keep your head up, eyes fixed straight ahead, shoulders back, back straight, and your weight on the entire foot throughout the upward and downward movement phases of this exercise.

Tips and Modifications:

- Knee pain in lower squat positions: Abbreviate descent to permit pain-free squat action.

- Excess tension on knees, feet, and Achilles tendon as indicated by heels lifting off the floor: With chest out, move your hips backward as well as downward on descent to keep your knees directly above your feet and your heels flat on the floor.

- Discomfort in shoulders, arms or hands: Hold the dumbbells on your shoulders rather than beside your hips.

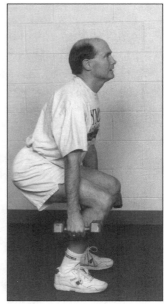

BACK EXTENSION

Focus: Erector spinae

Beginning Position:

1. Lie face down on a mat or carpeted floor.
2. Place your hands loosely behind your head.
3. A weight plate may be held behind the head for added resistance.

Upward Movement:

1. Raise your chest slowly about 30 degrees off the floor until the low back muscles are fully contracted.
2. Keep your hips on the floor at all times.
3. Exhale throughout the upward movement.

Downward Movement Phase:

1. Lower your chest to the floor slowly.
2. Inhale throughout the lowering movement.

Tips and Modifications:

- Inability to lift chest off the floor: Secure your feet to provide an anchor for trunk extension movement, or place your hands by your shoulders and use your arms to assist the low back muscles as in a modified push-up.

- Discomfort in low back area: Limit the lifting action to the pain-free range of movement or place your hands by your shoulders and use your arms to assist the low back muscles, as in a modified push-up.

- Strain in neck area: Maintain a neutral head position throughout the exercise.

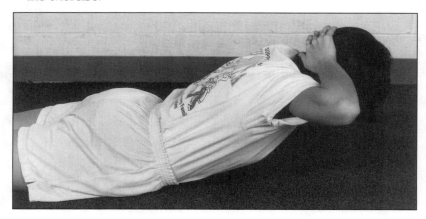

TRUNK CURL

Focus: Rectus abdominis

Beginning Position:

1. Lie on your back on a mat or carpeted floor.
2. Flex your knees to 110 degrees, feet flat on the floor.
3. Place your hands loosely behind your head to maintain a neutral neck position.
4. A weight plate may be held behind the head for added resistance.

Upward Movement Phase:

1. Raise your shoulders slowly about 30 degrees off the floor until your abdominal muscles are fully contracted.
2. Exhale throughout the upward movement.

Downward Movement Phase:

1. Lower your shoulders slowly to the floor.
2. Inhale throughout the lowering movement.

Tips and Modifications:

- Discomfort in low back area: Bring your feet closer to your hips to increase hip flexion and decrease arch in the low back area.
- Strain in neck area: Maintain a neutral head position throughout the exercise.

TRUNK CURL WITH TWIST

Focus: Rectus abdominis, external obliques, internal obliques

Beginning Position:

1.   Lie on your back on a mat or carpeted floor.

2.   Flex your knees to 110 degrees, feet flat on the floor.

3.   Place your hands loosely behind your head to maintain a neutral neck position.

4.   A weight may be held behind the head for added resistance.

Upward Movement Phase:

1.   Raise your shoulders slowly about 30 degrees off the floor until your abdominal muscles are fully contracted.

2.   At the end of the curl-up movement, twist your torso to the left as if to touch the right elbow to the left knee.

3.   Alternate twisting the torso to the left and to the right with every other curl-up.

4.   Exhale throughout the upward movement.

Downward Movement Phase:

1.   Lower your shoulders slowly to the floor.

2.   Inhale throughout the lowering movement.

Tips and Modifications:

- Discomfort in low back area: Bring your feet closer to your hips to increase hip flexion and decrease arch in the low back area.

- Strain in neck area: Maintain a neutral head position throughout the exercise.

- Stress in shoulders: Twist the entire torso a few degrees at the end of the curl-up movement rather than overturning with the shoulders.

DUMBBELL BENCH PRESS

Focus: Pectoralis major, anterior deltoid, triceps

Beginning Position:

1. Lie on your back with your legs straddling a bench, knees flexed at 90 degrees, feet flat on the floor.

2. Keep your head, shoulders, and buttocks in contact with the bench and your feet in contact with the floor throughout the exercise.

3. Grasp the dumbbells so your palms face away and push upwards until your arms are fully extended above your chest.

Downward Movement Phase:

1. Lower the dumbbells slowly in unison to the outside of your chest.

2. Inhale throughout the lowering movement.

Upward Movement Phase:

1. Press dumbbells upward in unison until your arms are fully extended.

2. Exhale throughout the upward movement.

Tips and Modifications:

- Pain in shoulders: Reduce the downward movement range and keep the dumbbells above your shoulders throughout each repetition.

- Discomfort in low back area: Place your feet on a stool to increase hip flexion and decrease arch in the low back.

DUMBBELL ONE-ARM BENT ROW

Focus: Latissimus dorsi, biceps

Beginning Position:

1. Grasp a dumbbell with your right hand and support your body weight by placing your left hand and knee on the bench, keeping your right leg straight and your right foot flat on the floor.

2. Position the dumbbell so that your arm is straight and your palm faces the bench.

3. Keep your back flat throughout exercise.

Upward Movement Phase:

1. Pull the dumbbell slowly to your chest.

2. Exhale throughout the pulling movement.

Downward Movement Phase:

1. Lower the dumbbell slowly to the starting position.

2. Inhale throughout the lowering movement.

3. Repeat the exercise from the beginning position with your left arm.

Tips and Modifications:

- Pain in shoulder area: Keep your upper arm close to your side throughout the exercise and do not allow your shoulder to be pulled downward.

- Discomfort in low back area: Place your knee directly under your hip and your hand directly under your shoulder to provide a solid base of back support. Keep your shoulders level throughout each repetition.

DUMBBELL LATERAL RAISE

Focus: Deltoids

Beginning Position:

1. Grasp the dumbbells with your palms facing the outside of your thighs and your elbows slightly flexed.
2. Stand erect with your feet hip-width apart.

Upward Movement Phase:

1. Lift the dumbbells slowly upward and sideward in unison until level with your shoulders, arms parallel to the floor.
2. Exhale throughout the upward movement.

Downward Movement Phase:

1. Lower the dumbbells slowly in unison to the starting position.
2. Inhale throughout the lowering movement.

Tips and Modifications:

- Pain in shoulders: Stop upward movement before your upper arms are parallel to the floor.
- Pain in wrists: Maintain a neutral wrist position throughout each repetition.
- Strain in elbows: Keep your elbows partially flexed throughout the exercise.

DUMBBELL CURL

Focus: Biceps

Beginning Position:

1. Grasp the dumbbells with your palms facing your outer thighs, arms straight. Make sure that your upper arms remain perpendicular to the floor and against your sides throughout this exercise.

2. Stand erect with your feet about hip-width apart and parallel to one another.

Upward Movement Phase:

1. Curl the dumbbells upward toward your shoulders, rotating your wrists until your palms face the chest.

2. Exhale throughout the upward movement.

Downward Movement Phase:

1. Lower dumbbells slowly in unison to the starting position.

2. Inhale throughout the lowering movement.

Tips and Modifications:

- Stress in shoulder area: Keep your upper arms firmly pressed against your sides throughout each repetition.

- Discomfort in low back area: Maintain an erect posture throughout the exercise, with no backward lean during the curling action.

- Pain in wrists: Keep your wrists in a neutral position at all times.

- Pain in elbow area: Reduce rotation of the forearms during lifting movement.

DUMBBELL OVERHEAD TRICEPS EXTENSION

Focus: Triceps

Beginning Position:

1. Grasp one dumbbell with both hands and sit erect with your feet about hip-width apart.

2. Lift the dumbbell upward until your arms are fully extended, directly above your head. Keep your upper arms perpendicular to the floor throughout exercise.

Downward Movement Phase:

1. Lower the dumbbell slowly toward the base of your neck.

2. Inhale throughout the lowering movement.

Upward Movement Phase:

1. Lift the dumbbell upward slowly until your arms are fully extended.

2. Exhale throughout lifting movement.

Tips and Modifications:

- Pain in shoulder area: Substitute the machine triceps extension or another triceps exercise performed below shoulder level.

- Discomfort in low back area: Maintain an erect posture throughout the exercise without excessive back arch.

- Pain in elbows: Keep your elbows high and near your head throughout each repetition and use abbreviated lowering movements.

- Pain in wrists: Keep your wrists in a neutral position at all times.

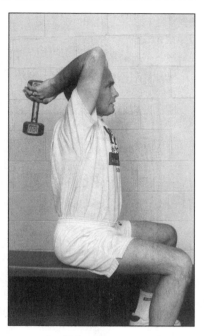

DUMBBELL WRIST CURL

Focus: Wrist flexors

Beginning Position:

1. Sit on a bench with the backs of your forearms resting securely on your thighs.

2. Hold the dumbbells loosely with an underhand grip.

Upward Movement Phase:

1. Curl the dumbbells slowly upward as far as possible without lifting your forearms off your thighs.

2. Exhale throughout the upward movement.

Downward Movement Phase:

1. Lower the dumbbells slowly until your wrists are fully extended.

2. Inhale throughout the lowering movement.

Tips and Modifications:

- Discomfort in wrists or forearms: Abbreviate the curling action to a pain-free range of movement.

DUMBBELL WRIST EXTENSION

Focus: Wrist extensors

Beginning Position:

1. Sit on a bench with the fronts of your forearms resting securely on your thighs.
2. Hold the dumbbells loosely with an overhand grip.

Upward Movement Phase:

1. Move the dumbbells upward slowly as far as possible without lifting your forearms off your thighs.
2. Exhale throughout the upward movement.

Downward Movement Phase:

1. Lower the dumbbells slowly until your wrists are fully flexed.
2. Inhale throughout the lowering movement.

Tips and Modifications:

- Discomfort in wrists or forearms: Abbreviate the lifting action to a pain-free range of movement.

THE NEXT STEP

Comprehensive muscular development is the first step toward improving your golf game and avoiding physical setbacks. The second step is to do more specialized stretching, strengthening, and sequencing exercises that take your golfing abilities to higher performance levels. The remaining chapters of this book present a well-tested program of sport-specific exercises that should definitely increase your driving distance, injury resistance, and playing enjoyment. For best results, use a combination of both isolated and integrated strength programs. The golf training programs in chapter 8 provide a variety of training programs based on equipment availability, season of year, schedule time available, physical limitations, and competitive level.

CHAPTER 5

POSTURAL STABILITY FOR A CONSISTENT SWING PLANE

The most important rule in a golf conditioning program is to work and develop strength from the core region of the body outward. A strong trunk allows forces to be transferred effectively from the legs to the upper body during activities in which kinetic linking is required. It also bolsters the body to withstand those forces without breakdown. Once you have achieved a reasonably high level of overall muscular strength, the next step is postural stability through sensible midsection training.

Greg Norman has benefited from the development of core strength for stabilization. His individualized program consists of isolating the lower part of the abdominal region, the oblique musculature, as well as the upper abdominal muscles. A lower back strengthening program is also extremely important in Greg's case, because postural stability allows the golfer to maintain the spine angle throughout the entire swing. Greg's history of low back problems made it imperative that his trunk strength become the focus of his training. Fortunately, Greg is a disciplined athlete with a work ethic that matches his tremendous talent. The main focus of his program was trunk stabilization, with another primary focus on his lower body region. The upper body is the third priority after the trunk and lower body. Greg experienced the benefits of his core strength development every time he golfed, and you can, too.

POSTURE MEANS POWER

Believe it or not, posture has a positive influence on power production. Just as it is impossible to run fast without proper posture, it is unwise to swing a golf club without appropriate postural stability. Functional posture makes a world of difference in your swinging action and lets you impart far more force in your ball strike. For a simple demonstration, try sitting slumped in a chair with your head pushed forward. Now try to raise your arm. Now try to turn your head to the left, as you would have to do during the backswing. Now try to turn your body to the right. Next, sit up straight with your chin pulled in and your back slightly arched. Repeat the above motions and then decide which posture produced a greater range of motion.

Body structure and posture are individual characteristics, but an improper golf swing can cause certain muscle imbalances. These imbalances might not be obvious until they cause a disruptive physical problem. Some common physical limitations include:

- Reduced neck rotation can make it difficult to keep your eye on the ball during the swing.

- Insufficient trunk strength interferes with your ability to transfer forces from the lower body to the upper body. In addition, proper spine angle will not be maintained during the swing.

- Tight hamstrings do not allow an effective address position to be achieved.

- Reduced range of hip motion leads to compromised swing patterns.

- Decreased trunk rotation limits shoulder turn and causes poor sequencing between the hips and trunk region.

- Insufficient shoulder strength, especially in the rotator cuff, leads to decreased club head speed, as well as poor deceleration and club control.

Many players think of these problems as a mere product of the sport and resort to anti-inflammatory medication and other quick-fix alternatives. These responses might reduce pain temporarily, but they rarely solve the underlying problem. Most postural conditions do not occur overnight. The body slowly adapts to poor posture, and some body parts, like the neck, shoulder, back, and hip, may be overused to compensate for loss of motion someplace else. By performing a few simple exercises regularly, however, you can improve and maintain good posture and thereby improve your swinging power.

The ability to maintain your functional trunk position for each shot is an acquired skill. Teaching pros commonly refer to this position as *maintaining spine angle.* When the spine is stable it serves as an efficient and rigid lever to transfer energy from the lower body to the upper body. By increasing the stability of the spine and the muscles that support it, you therefore can improve your game.

© Action Images

Mark O'Meara hired a physical therapist the year he won two majors at age 41.

Bending the spine places unnecessary stress on the lower back muscles and joints. It also reduces your ability to transfer power from your lower body to your upper body, which translates into decreased club head speed. For example, when your upper back is bent forward or hunched over, you place extra stress on your shoulders and neck as your shoulders round forward, thereby causing the rotator cuff muscles (a group of four small muscles that protect the shoulder joint) to work in an abnormal position. This undesirable posture can produce tendonitis, muscle strain, and joint sprain by placing the muscles at a mechanical disadvantage. Of course, this position also limits your swing action to a portion of the potential movement range.

Postural muscles (the muscles that maintain spine angle) are found throughout the body and function more for endurance than for strength or power. The main role of these muscles is to hold the skeletal system and joint structures in proper alignment so the larger and stronger muscles can produce the desired body movements with appropriate forces in tandem with keeping good balance.

If you ever stood at the loop at St. Andrews and felt the wind blow, you know the importance of balance. Balance is one of the golfer's key

Efficient leverage.   **Stress-inducing approach.**

fitness components. The balancing interactions of the body represent a complex communication system. Balance is controlled by the central nervous system, the eyes, the inner ear, and tiny message receptors in the joints and soft tissues. When the ball lies uphill, downhill, level or side hill, above or below the feet, poor balance definitely can contribute to a poor shot from an imperfect lie. If we combine these factors with an inability to maintain proper trunk position throughout the swing, we increase both the probability of a poor shot and a physical injury. The goal of the postural exercise program is to improve both static and dynamic balance for the purpose of developing functional stability during the swing.

MUSCLE BALANCE PATTERNS

Respected practicing physician Vladimir Janda, a Finnish physician, categorized various muscles into two types of functional groups, namely those prone to tightness (those not bold on pages 94 and 95), and those prone to weakness (those in bold type on pages 94 and 95).

Muscles prone to tightness largely have to do with posture, whereas muscles prone to weakness are those that have other functions. Janda's work has proven extremely beneficial in determining postural imbalances that can make it difficult to maintain a desirable position during the golf swing. You want to avoid this problem, of course, so that your swinging action can be as powerful and productive as possible.

STRENGTHENING YOUR POSTURAL MUSCLES

Because the body must work as a unit during the golf swing, functional training programs should include multijoint strengthening exercises such as the following exercises. For example, shoulder motion might be influenced by restrictions found in the midback muscles and joints. Likewise, restrictions in the lower back might be influenced by problems in the hip region. This is the reason posture should be assessed for the entire body and not just the area that appears to be inhibiting the swing. Remember that perfect posture is created through a perfect combination of mobility (see chapter 3) and stability (see chapter 4). Factors that contribute to mobility and stability include strength training, flexibility training, balance training, and motor learning.

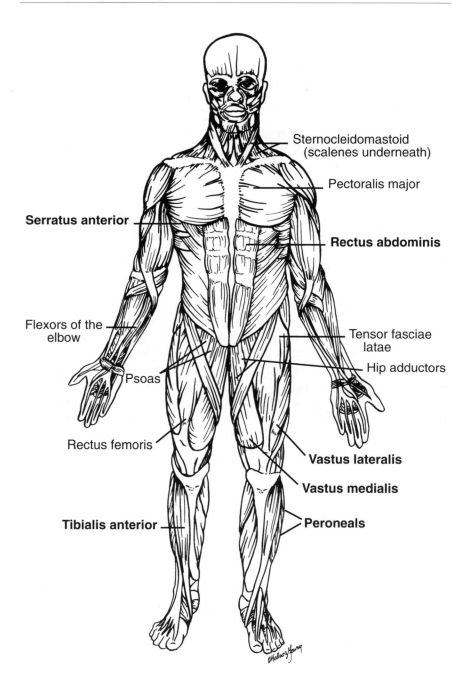

Sternocleidomastoid
(scalenes underneath)

Pectoralis major

Serratus anterior

Rectus abdominis

Flexors of the
elbow

Tensor fasciae
latae

Hip adductors

Psoas

Rectus femoris

Vastus lateralis

Vastus medialis

Tibialis anterior

Peroneals

Muscles in boldface type are prone to weakness.

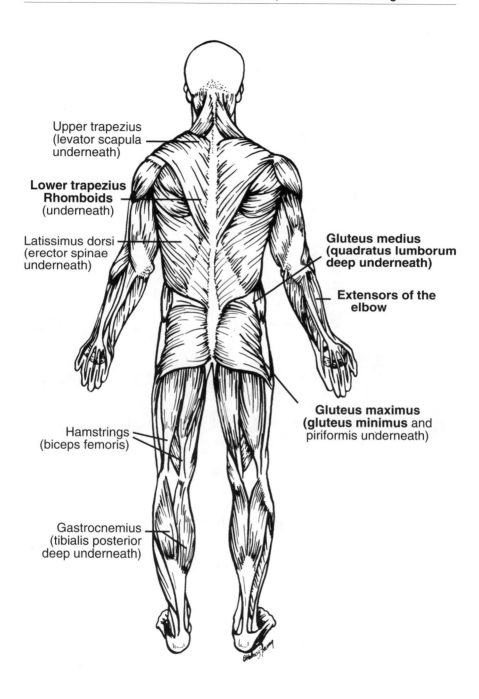

Upper trapezius
(levator scapula
underneath)

**Lower trapezius
Rhomboids**
(underneath)

Latissimus dorsi
(erector spinae
underneath)

**Gluteus medius
(quadratus lumborum
deep underneath)**

**Extensors of the
elbow**

**Gluteus maximus
(gluteus minimus** and
piriformis underneath)

Hamstrings
(biceps femoris)

Gastrocnemius
(tibialis posterior
deep underneath)

Muscles in boldface type are prone to weakness.

Conventional conditioning typically neglects strengthening the postural muscles, but training these muscles is necessary to keep imbalances from occurring. Exercises for postural muscles are performed with less resistance and more repetitions than exercises for the major muscle groups. The following is a basic training program for the low back and abdominal muscles. Remember that strength must be developed in the trunk area before you can produce consistent, efficient, and safe golf swings.

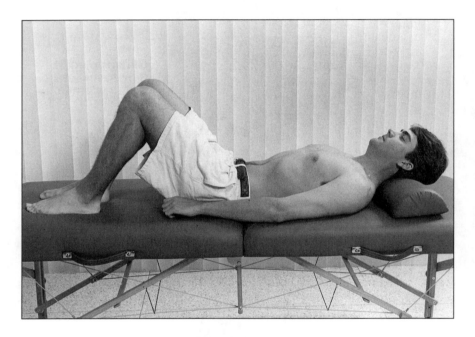

ABDOMINAL HOLLOWING

Focus: Abdominal muscles and trunk stabilizers

Procedure:

1. Lie on your back with your head supported and your knees bent. Rest your feet firmly on the floor.

2. Slowly pull your stomach up beneath your rib cage and hold for 2 to 3 seconds.

3. Remain stable, without moving the pelvis or the spine, while doing this deep abdominal contraction.

Volume: 10 to 15 repetitions

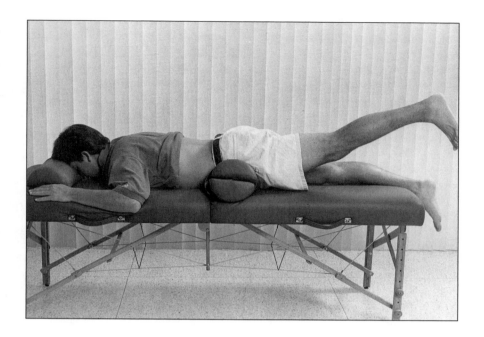

PRONE LEG RAISE

Focus: Gluteal and lower back muscles

Procedure:

1. Lie down on your abdominal region. You may place a pillow under your abdominal muscles for support, especially if you feel pain in the low back when lying down.

2. Squeezing your buttocks, raise one leg approximately 6 to 16 inches off the floor.

3. Keep your body still and hold for 2 seconds.

4. Repeat on the opposite side.

Volume: 10 repetitions

Tip: Squeezing the buttocks together will provide better stability for superimposing the hip movement.

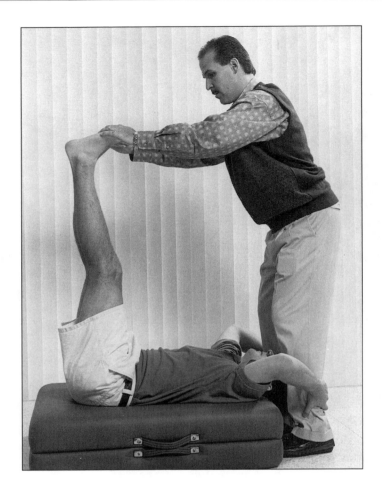

LEG PUSH DOWN

Focus: Lower abdominal muscles and hip flexors

Procedure:

1. Lie on your back with your head supported and your knees bent.
2. Place your hands around the ankles of a person standing above you.
3. Raise both legs straight in the air.
4. While your legs are raised, the partner attempts to push your legs toward the ground. Resist your partner's push but do not throw the legs down.

Volume: 10 to 15 repetitions

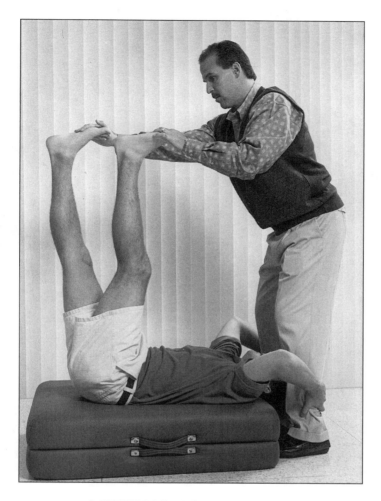

ALTERNATING LEG PUSH

Focus: Abdominal muscles and hip flexors

Procedure:

1. Lie on your back with your head supported.
2. Place your hands around the ankles of a person standing above you.
3. Raise both legs in the air, keeping your knees straight.
4. While your legs are straight and in the air, the partner attempts to push one leg toward the ground. Resist your partner's push.
5. Have partner repeat with the other leg.

Volume: 10 to 15 repetitions each leg

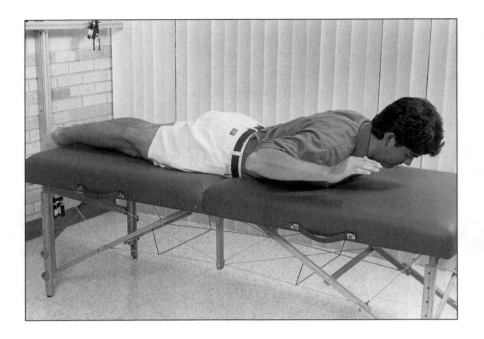

COBRA

Focus: Develop strength of midback region while low back is isometrically contracted.

Procedure:

1. Lie face down with a pillow placed beneath your abdomen, if desired.

2. Squeeze your buttocks and your shoulder blades. Then raise your upper body off the floor.

3. Hold for 2 seconds keeping your buttocks contracted until you lower your body back to the floor.

Volume: 10 to 15 repetitions

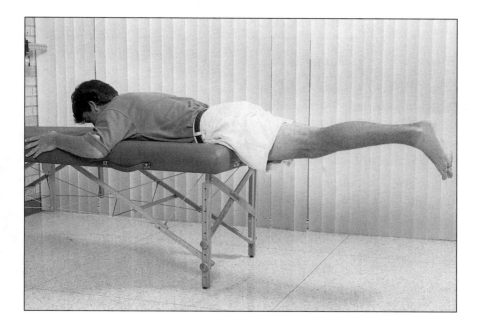

DOUBLE LEG RAISE

Focus: Gluteal, lower back muscles, and hamstrings

Procedure:

1. Lie face down on a stabilization ball or exercise table such that your lower body from the hips down is hanging off the table.

2. Tighten your midsection muscles and raise your legs off the ground until they are parallel to the floor.

3. Hold for 2 to 3 seconds and lower them back to the floor. Repeat.

Volume: 10 to 15 repetitions

BACK HYPER

Focus: Lower back muscles

Procedure:

1.   Lie on top of a stabilization ball so that your abdomen rests on the ball with arms supporting your body.

2.   Place your hands on your chest and initiate movement by squeezing the buttocks together.

3.   Raise your upper body off the ball and hold for 2 to 3 seconds.

Volume: 10 to 15 repetitions

SOLO TWIST

Focus: Lower back and abdominal muscles

Procedure:

1.   Sit on floor with your legs straight out in front.

2.   Hold a medicine ball behind your back.

3.   Rotate to one side and pick up the ball with both hands.

4.   Holding the ball, rotate to the other side and place the ball behind your back.

Volume: 8 repetitions in each direction

RUSSIAN TWIST SIT-UP

Focus: Lower back and abdominal muscles

Procedure:

1.   Lie on your back with your head supported and your knees bent. Rest your feet firmly on the floor.

2.   Raise a light weight or medicine ball above your chest.

3.   Perform a sit-up. While keeping your trunk stable, rotate your shoulders to one side and then the other.

4.   After rotating to each side, lie back down.

Volume: 8 repetitions

Postural Positions

Keep in mind that your everyday postural positions also contribute to muscle tightness and muscle weakness. For example, a swayback position, also known as *lordosis,* is associated with tight low back muscles, whereas a humped back posture, commonly referred to as *kyphosis,* is associated with weak low back muscles. A forward head and shoulders posture places undesirable stress on the neck muscles, and a curved spine posture, called *scoliosis,* results in tight muscles on the shorter side and weak muscles on the longer side of the back.

UNLOADED PROGRAM

There might be days when you already have hit many balls and thus have subjected your spine to tremendous stress. On such days, consider supplementing your workout with exercises in an unloaded position, that is, one in which you minimize the forces that compress the spine when standing or sitting. The unloaded program provides a safe, minimal impact alternative for exercising the trunk muscles without missing a scheduled workout. Aerobic conditioning in a pool also can provide an opportunity for low-impact conditioning. In addition to the following exercises, perform the abdominal hollowing (p. 96), prone leg raise (p. 97), cobra (p. 100), and double leg raise (p. 101) in the unloaded program.

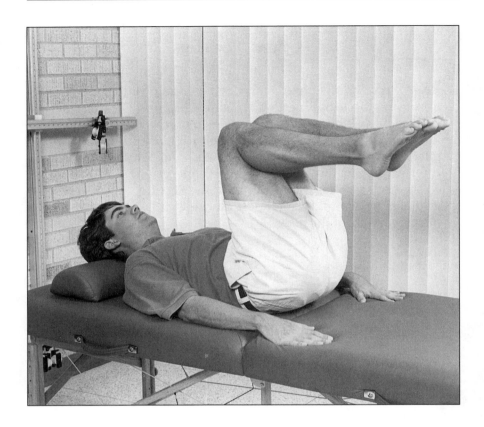

KNEES TO CEILING

Focus: Lower abdominal muscles

Procedure:

1. Lie flat on your back with your head supported.
2. Place your feet on floor and raise your legs toward your chest, above your waist.
3. Keep your knees bent and imagine that a piece of string is attached to each knee.
4. Visualize the strings lifting the knees directly toward the ceiling.
5. Hold knees up for 2 to 3 seconds before lowering.

Volume: 10 to 15 repetitions

Tip: If you must start with your knees already bent, then this exercise might be too difficult for you.

WHEELBARROW

Focus: Back and trunk muscles (stabilization)

Procedure:

1. Kneel on the ground with your forearms resting on the stabilization ball. Keep your back straight.

2. Rise up, off your knees, and roll forward on the ball, maintaining trunk stability.

3. Hold for at least 5 seconds.

Volume: Start with 10×5 seconds; build to 4×30 seconds

Tip: Do not let your trunk sag or bow.

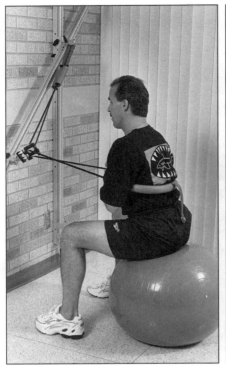 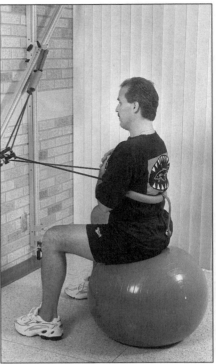

TUBING BACK EXTENSION

Focus: Lower and midback muscles

Procedure:

1. Sit on a stabilization ball with your feet planted on the ground.
2. Place tubing in the bottom of the door with the waist belt wrapped around your back.
3. Move away from the anchoring point until tension is created in the tubing.
4. Lean forward, hinging at the hips, and extend back.

Volume: 2×20 repetitions

Tip: To increase difficulty, raise the tubing above the chest level, but keep it below the armpits.

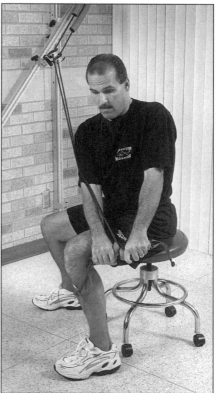

SEATED CHOP

Focus: Shoulder and trunk muscles

Procedure:

1. Anchor tubing high on a door.

2. Sit on a chair with one side toward the anchoring point.

3. Create some tension in the tubing.

4. Pull the tubing toward your chest with thumbs facing down.

5. When you reach the sternum, push the tubing away.

6. The movement is a diagonal pattern from above the shoulder to the chest, to below the waist, in the direction of the hip, to the opposite side of the body.

Volume: 12 repetitions each way

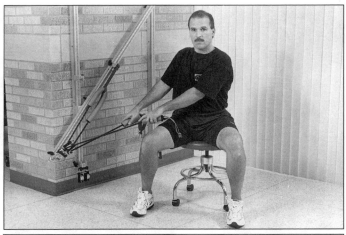

SEATED LIFT

Focus: Shoulder and trunk muscles

Procedure:

1. Anchor tubing low on the door.

2. Sit on a chair with one side toward the anchoring point. Keep the spine neutral.

3. Pull the tubing toward your chest with the thumbs pointed down.

4. The movement is a diagonal pattern from below the waist, to the chest, to above the shoulder, in the direction of the shoulder, on the opposite side of the body.

Volume: 12 repetitions each way

LATERAL GLIDE

Focus: Trunk muscles

Procedure:

1. Lie on your back with your legs resting on a stabilization ball and your upper body resting on some exercise mats.
2. Form a bridge with buttocks off the floor.
3. Use your abdominal and lower back muscles to move ball first to the right and then to the left.
4. Perform the movement in a controlled manner.

Volume: 8 repetitions each side

THE NEXT STEP

It is important to build your strength from the core of the body outward to the extremities. In golf, trunk strength and stability are essential for maintaining spine angle throughout the swing. Trunk stability not only insures against injury but is also an important component of motor learning. Successfully conditioning the nervous system to repeatedly perform the same swing movement requires consistent sequencing of the individual body parts. If your spine angle changes from shot to shot due to weakness of the trunk muscles, you will not be able to learn and replicate your best swing. Strengthening and stabilizing the trunk muscles provides you with the opportunity to develop a consistent and reproducible golf swing.

Once you have established a solid postural base, you are ready to elevate your game to the next level with improved swing sequence coordination. Chapter 6 shows you how to master the sequential segments of the golf swing for greater power transfer and more effective swing execution.

COORDINATION FOR POWER TRANSFER AND SKILL EXECUTION

Tom Watson continues to win on the PGA Tour. Each week he competes against players half his age. His ball striking ability is still one of the best on the tour. Although he has lost some driving distance, compared to 10 years ago, he continues to drive the ball an exceptionally long way. At the 1994 US Open played at Oakmont, Tom was paired with two very long hitters during one of the rounds. On a short, uphill par four that measured a little over 300 yards, several players had tried unsuccessfully to reach the green off the tee. The one player who had the length and accuracy to put his tee shot on the edge of the green was Tom Watson. Tom was 44 years old then. When you look at his build, you wouldn't think that he could hit the ball that far, but his superb swing sequence enables him to generate exceptional power for his body type and size. Sequencing of the swing with efficiency and power is much more important than absolute strength.

We define movement as a series of repeated muscular contractions regulated by the nervous system and directed by motor learning pathways. Purposeful movement depends on intimate communication among all the mechanisms that regulate muscle length and tension. In athletics, success depends on the speed and sequence at which these impulses are transmitted to achieve the desired body action. Because all movements in both competitive athletics and normal daily activities involve a repeated series of muscle stretch and shortening cycles, specific functional exercise best prepares the individual for the activity.

The central nervous system processes information provided through five basic sensory analyzers:

1. *Proprioceptive* or body awareness
2. *Tactile* or sense of touch
3. *Vestibular* or balance and equilibrium
4. *Optic* or visual
5. *Acoustic* or auditory

At least three of these information processing and feedback systems—body awareness, balance, and visual focus—are important factors in developing a productive and reproducible golf swing.

THE GOLF SWING

For players at every level, the golf swing is one of the most difficult skills to execute consistently because it requires a high degree of spatial awareness for the ever-changing conditions of play. Of course, temporal problems, abnormal joint mechanics, soft tissue restriction, poor posture, strength, flexibility, coordination, or balance also can have adverse affects on swing consistency and effectiveness. Because all of these factors enter into skill reproduction, it is easy to see why a person might shoot a score of 78 on one day and 94 on another. Because high-velocity movements require immediate responses to sensory input, reproduction of the ideal golf swing becomes most difficult.

Learning a new skill or improving an old one relies on carefully identifying your problem areas. Once you are aware of your problem areas, you can do something to correct them. You begin to excel when action becomes reaction.

A solid golf swing must be built on a solid neuromuscular foundation, which is why it is important to understand postural stability. As was discussed in chapter 5, postural stability is built upon the foundation of

LPGA young superstar Karrie Webb.

lower body mechanics. Actions of the lower body are composed of both linear and rotational components, and it is the proper interaction of these two movements that create a stable basis for the golf swing.

Defining the Forces

Your feet generate forces when they push against the ground. These forces act to propel your body and create motion. Two types of forces are important to the golf swing: *normal* forces and *shear* forces. Normal forces are illustrated in the linear components of the swing, and shear forces are illustrated in the rotational components of the swing.

Normal forces are applied by the feet downward or perpendicular to the ground. Weight is transferred to the back foot during the backswing and to the front foot during the downswing. When weight is shifted to one foot, the amount of force supplied by the foot increases while the normal force applied by the other foot decreases. This action defines the linear component of the movement. The linear movement of the body during the golf swing is very important because it is from this movement that the body develops momentum that enhances the rotational speed and power of the hips.

Shear force is applied by the feet along the surface of, or parallel to, the ground. Through the swing, shear forces are being applied by both feet. These shear forces create torque that turns the hips around the axis of the trunk as shown in the figure below. This defines the rotational component of the lower body movement. The rotational component can be related most directly to the ultimate club head speed attained in the swing.

When faults occur in lower body mechanics, the effect on the golf swing is analogous to cracks in the foundation of a house. When a stable base is lost, swing efficiency erodes. The most common fault in lower body mechanics is *sliding*. When a golfer slides, the interaction between the linear and rotational components breaks down, weight transfer is diminished, and rotation is lost.

Developing Muscular Awareness

The following drills are used to help develop muscular coordination and awareness of our body movements. Do not mistake these drills for golf swing technique drills and do not hit balls when performing these drills.

LINEAR WEIGHT TRANSFER

Focus: To become accustomed to appropriate weight transfer

Procedure:

1. Assume a golf stance in front of a mirror.
2. Shift approximately 80 percent of your weight to the rear foot (called *loaded position*).
3. Rotate, loading on the back leg, keeping the upper body in the backswing position as you rotate your hips to initiate the motion.
4. Hold and feel the position.
5. Transfer weight slowly from the rear to front foot, ending with approximately 80 percent weight on the front foot.

Tips:

- Feel the weight transfer.
- Make sure you are hinging at the hips and not bending at the back.
- Do not slide the hips out from under the shoulders.

ROTATIONAL WEIGHT TRANSFER

Focus: To drill simultaneously for proper rotation and weight transfer

Procedure:

1. Assume a golf stance in front of a mirror.
2. Shift approximately 80 percent of your weight to the rear foot.
3. Now rotate segments approximately 45 degrees in a clockwise direction (loaded position). Start with the hips-trunk segment, then the trunk-shoulders, and finally the shoulders-arms.
4. Hold and feel the position.
5. Transfer weight slowly from the rear to front foot and rotate in a counterclockwise direction. End with about 90 percent of the weight on the front foot.

Tips:

- Check your alignment through the entire motion. Always keep the shoulders directly above the hips.
- Make sure you are hinging at the hips and not bending at the back.
- Make sure rotation and weight transfer occur simultaneously.

Energy Transfer

No specific link of the golf swing can be singled out as more important than any other. Your swing is only as strong as your weakest link, however. During the golf swing, the transfer of energy and power from the lower body to the upper body is the most pivotal link and the most common weakness observed in recreational golfers. The role of the trunk musculature in the golf swing is much like the role of the crankshaft in automobile performance. Just as the crankshaft turns power created by the pistons into torque at the drive wheels, the trunk musculature turns power created by the lower body into torque at the upper body, which in turn creates club head speed. With maximum energy transfer comes maximum power.

During a right-handed golfer's backswing, the hip and shoulder segments rotate clockwise around the orientation of the spine. As this occurs, trunk musculature that connects the hip and shoulder segments begins to load as a result of the coiling action. This is important because the energy stored in the muscles during the loading process will help accelerate the shoulders during the swing. Even more important, however, is the dynamic interaction of the hip and shoulder segments. In other words, it is not just how much coil, but the timing and sequence that creates maximum power.

Maximum power is generated in the golf swing when the action of the lower body generates a counterclockwise acceleration of the hips around the axis of the spine. The hip segment accelerates first, creating a dynamic loading of the trunk musculature. The shoulder segment then follows the lead of the hip segment in a counterclockwise direction and accelerates. At this time the hip segment begins to decelerate. This action passes energy to the trunk as these muscles contract to accelerate the shoulder segment. The result is the creation of power and rotational speed of the shoulders, about double that of the hips.

The two most common breakdowns in transferring energy from the lower body to the upper body originate with the hip segment. The first of these is called *sliding hips,* which occurs when the hips move laterally to the left without rotating. No rotational speed is created. This actually diminishes energy that can be passed to the upper body. In many cases sliding hips also indicate an excessive spine tilt. When the spine tilts, muscles that work to rotate the segments around the axis of the trunk become asymmetrical in that one side shortens and the other side lengthens. This asymmetry causes inefficient generation of power and can increase stress on the low back and joint structures. The second problem is called *spinning hips,* which occurs when the golfer forces the hip segment through the swing too quickly. This creates an excessive lag between the lower body and the upper body, and the upper body typically does not catch up. The trunk musculature therefore is unable to pass energy created by the hip segment rotation to the shoulder segment rotation, which means lost power and slower club head speed.

The desired interaction between hip segment rotation and trunk segment rotation occurs in perfect sequence during the optimal swing. The key to this coordinated action is a high level of strength and flexibility through the trunk area, especially the muscles that contribute to trunk stabilization and rotary movements.

Coordinating Body Segments

Developing an effective power source for a productive swing depends on a fit body with well-conditioned muscles. The following drills should assist you in achieving better body segment coordination and power transfer during the golf swing. Be careful not to force rotation. Only rotate the shoulders to a position that can be obtained comfortably. No stress should be felt. If stress is perceived, discontinue the drill.

POWER ENERGY TRANSFER I

Focus: To become aware of power transferring from the hips to the upper body

Procedure:

1. Stand in front of a mirror.
2. Place your hands on your shoulders.
3. Rotate the shoulders in a clockwise direction.
4. Resist hip rotation.
5. Reach maximum shoulder rotation without forcing.
6. Hold the position for 2 seconds.
7. Rotate your shoulders in a counterclockwise direction back to neutral position.

Tip: Do this movement slowly, feeling the muscles of the trunk working to turn the shoulders.

POWER ENERGY TRANSFER II

Focus: To become aware of power transferring from the hips to the upper body

Procedure:

1. Stand in front of a mirror.
2. Place your hands on your shoulders.
3. Rotate the shoulders in a clockwise direction.
4. Resist hip rotation.
5. Reach maximum shoulder rotation without forcing.
6. Hold the position for 2 seconds.
7. Rotate your shoulders in a counterclockwise direction back to neutral position.
8. Continue a counterclockwise direction.
9. Release your hips and finish the rotation.

Tips:

- Do the movements slowly.
- Once you obtain a neutral position, release the hips and the motion is finished.

Club Release

It has been called *club release, wrist uncocking,* or *club lag.* What is really being discussed and how does it affect your swing? Club release or wrist uncocking refers to the angle made between the club shaft and the plane of the arms as they move around the axis of the trunk. In the downswing the golfer's arms drive down to the ball. Using energy created by the lower body and passed through the core region to the upper body, the arms achieve increased rotational speed. As the arms accelerate, the angle between the arms and the club shaft remains the same, in a cocked position. When the arms begin to decelerate, however, energy passes from the arms to the club, causing it to increase in rotational speed. The visual result is a change in the angle between club shaft and the arms, hence the phrase *club release* or *wrist uncocking.* If timed properly, the club accelerates to maximum velocity upon impact with the ball, resulting in optimum power production.

Club release is easily seen by the unaided eye as the increase in angle between the club shaft and the arms when the swing nears impact with the ball. Until now, however, we have not had the technology to measure and analyze this action objectively, causing the evolution of many erroneous explanations of the visual perception. Two common misconceptions are the benefits of holding the club in a cocked position until impact, or forcing the release by throwing the club from the top.

Holding the cocked position interferes with the action of the arms accelerating around the axis of the trunk and reduces club head speed. In reality, the action of the arms accelerating around the axis of the trunk is what creates the cocked angle and maintains that angle during the downswing. When the arms begin to decelerate, the club angle should increase into impact as the club accelerates. Tension in the muscles of the wrists and arms caused by trying to hold the cocked angle typically results in the disruption of the natural energy flow. This disruption creates a premature deceleration of the arms and consequently a premature release of the club angle, as well as increased stress in the upper body and arms. Be sure to avoid this mistake.

The other common misconception is throwing the club from the top. Again, the club achieves greatest acceleration when the arms decelerate and the cocked position automatically releases. Trying to force the release most often disrupts energy flow and creates tension in muscles, causing a premature deceleration of the arms and less impact power. Effective golf swings create and release the club angle with productive arm action. Productive arm action results from the following combination of sequential movements:

1. Power generation using the large muscles of the lower body.
2. Efficient transfer of energy from the legs through the core muscles to the upper body and shoulders.
3. Acceleration of the arms for optimum energy culmination and maximum power production.

Combatting Common Flaws

The most common flaw in generating power on impact is early club release, which basically boils down to inefficient linking and premature arm deceleration. To enhance your club release velocity and impact power, you must learn to accelerate the arms effectively. Effective arm action takes a combination of strength, flexibility, and swing technique. To best develop flexibility and strength components, refer to the exercises presented in chapters 3 and 4. Along with those exercises, the following drills help develop more effective arm action.

ARM ACCELERATION I

Focus: To drill the proper sequence of arm movements for productive swing action

Procedure:

1. Stand in front of a mirror.
2. Hold your arms straight out in front of your chest with your palms together.
3. Create a solid foundation: Isolate the muscles by resisting rotation of the hips.
4. Rotate the upper body, shoulders, and arms in a clockwise direction.
5. Reaching a maximum rotation position, accelerate the body in a counterclockwise direction.
6. Stop rotation in the neutral position.

Tips:

- Do this movement at a slow to moderate speed.
- Responsive acceleration of the arm is the function of the larger muscles sequentially passing energy from the lower body power base, through the core muscles, to the upper body and arms.

ARM ACCELERATION II

Focus: To drill the proper sequence of arm movements for productive swing action

Procedure:

1. Stand in front of a mirror.
2. Hold your arms straight out in front of your chest with your palms together.
3. Create a solid foundation: Isolate the muscles by resisting rotation of the hips.
4. Rotate the upper body, shoulders, and arms in a clockwise direction.
5. Reaching a maximum rotation position, accelerate the body in a counterclockwise direction.
6. Stop rotation in the neutral position and obtain neutral alignment.
7. Release hips to follow through.

Tip: Do not release the hips until a neutral alignment is obtained.

DEVELOPING YOUR SWING IMPROVEMENT PROGRAM

A successful preparatory program should be sequentially designed, follow an established strength base, and be supervised by an exercise professional with a scientific understanding and practical application of functional biomechanics and training progressions. The training program can include a variety of exercises, limited only by the creativeness of the conditioning specialist. Because year-round training for golf can lead to boredom and lack of motivation, every effort should be made to provide variety in the exercise program. If you do not have access to a golf fitness instructor (or even if you do), the training programs and protocols in this book should help you develop a high level of physical conditioning for better golf performance.

You can add variety to your program by using different pieces of equipment and different movement patterns. We provide skill training drills as well as power training programs utilizing weighted clubs, medicine balls, and tubing (see table 6.1). A well-designed training program is based on planning and progression; failing to plan is planning to fail.

The training program should result in a properly sequenced and well-timed golf swing. As Chris Welch of Human Performance Technologies and his fellow researchers have discovered, "Proper timing facilitates successfully higher rotational velocities." Furthermore, according to Welch and his coworkers, once a basic understanding of the correct golf swing is developed, you can begin to work on specific mechanical parameters of a more intricate nature.

Table 6.1   Power Program

Program part	Focus	Exercises
I. Warm-up	Connecting and disconnecting	Linear weight transfer Rotational weight transfer Power energy transfer (I and II) Arm acceleration (I and II)
II. Weight shift	Being aware of weight shift with movement through all planes of motion	Wood chopping Backward throw Russian twist Discus throw
III. Medicine ball training	Activating the stretch-shortening cycle	Overhead throw Chest pass Diagonal
	Improving rate of force development and intramuscular coordination	Backward throw Underhand throw Overhead throw Side pass
IV. Lower body	Improving rate of force development and intramuscular coordination	Bench jump Side box
V. Club training—long response (LR)		LR heavy baseball swing LR light golf swing LR standard golf swing
VI. Club training—short response (SR)	Speed and golf swing carryover	SR heavy baseball swing SR light golf swing SR standard golf swing

WARM-UP DRILLS

Perform the linear weight transfer and rotational weight transfer drills (pp. 115 and 116) for 30 seconds each to warm up your weight transfer awareness as well as the muscles of your midsection and lower back. You can vary these drills also by doing them while holding a basketball or medicine ball. Finish the warm-up with the power energy transfer I and II drills (pp. 119 and 120) and the arm acceleration I and II drills (pp. 123 and 124). The warm-up drills were first seen in Vern Gambetta and Steve Odgers' *The Complete Guide to Medicine Ball Training*.

WEIGHT SHIFT DRILLS

WOOD CHOPPING

Focus: To promote dynamic movement of flexion of the trunk

Procedure:

1. Straddle with your knees slightly flexed, your upper body erect, and the ball held overhead.
2. Swing the ball forward and down in a chopping motion.
3. Let the ball swing between the legs and return to the starting position.

Duration: 20 to 30 seconds

Tip: Move in a controlled manner.

BACKWARD THROW WARM-UP

Focus: To promote dynamic movement of extension of the trunk

Procedure:

1. Holding a medicine ball, straddle with your knees slightly flexed and the upper body erect.
2. Hinge at the hips while holding the ball out from your chest.
3. Bend backward to no more than 90 degrees and return torso to starting position, extending arms overhead.

Duration: 20 to 30 seconds

Tip: Move in a controlled manner.

STANDING RUSSIAN TWIST

Focus: To promote dynamic rotation of the trunk

Procedure:

1. Straddle-stand with your knees slightly flexed while the ball is held away from your body.

2. Alternate twisting to the right and left, being sure to start slowly and increase speed only after you become familiar with the exercise.

Duration: 20 to 30 seconds

Tip: Move in a controlled manner.

DISCUS THROW

Focus: To promote dynamic movement in diagonal fashion

Procedure:

1. Straddle-stand with the ball held no higher than waist position.
2. Bend your knees and swing the ball from starting position to the direction of the opposite shoulder.

Duration: 20 to 30 seconds in each direction

Tip: This exercise movement is much like the movement in throwing a discus.

MEDICINE BALL EXERCISES

SEATED OVERHEAD THROW

Focus: To activate the stretch-shortening cycle

Procedure:

1. Sit on a flat bench or stabilization ball.
2. Hold a medicine ball over your head with arms extended.
3. Extend arms backward to initiate forward throw of ball.

Volume: 10 repetitions

Tip: Use the flat bench for this throw until you have strengthened your trunk. Once you have sufficient trunk stability perform the throw while sitting on a stabilization ball.

SEATED CHEST PASS

Focus: To activate the stretch-shortening cycle

Procedure:

1. Sit on a stabilization ball or flat bench about 10 feet away from a partner.
2. Sit with your feet shoulder-width apart.
3. Hold a medicine ball at your chest with both hands.
4. Pass the ball to the partner by extending both arms forward.

Volume: 1 to 2 × 10 repetitions

DIAGONAL

Focus: To activate the stretch-shortening cycle

Procedure:

1. Sit on a stabilization ball or flat bench.
2. Hold a medicine ball with both hands.
3. Initiating the movement from one side of your body, pass the ball across your body diagonally.

Volume: 10 repetitions

BACKWARD THROW

Focus: To improve the rate of force development and intramuscular coordination

Procedure:

1. Stand in a straddle position with the medicine ball held extended overhead.
2. Swing the ball down between your legs while simultaneously squatting and bending at the waist.
3. Explode back up and throw the ball back over your head for maximum distance.

Volume: 5 to 10 repetitions

UNDERHAND THROW

Focus: To improve the rate of force development and intramuscular coordination

Procedure:

1. Swing the medicine ball down between your legs, simultaneously bending at the knees and hips.
2. Extend the hips, legs, and back, throwing the ball forward for maximum distance.

Volume: 5 to 10 repetitions

OVERHEAD THROW

Focus: To improve the rate of force development and intramuscular coordination

Procedure:

1. Straddle-stand, with your knees slightly flexed and your back arched, holding the medicine ball overhead with elbows flexed.
2. Extend the legs and the arms.
3. Throw the ball forward, against a wall.

Volume: 5 to 10 repetitions

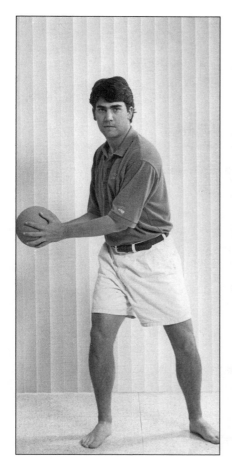 

SIDE PASS

Focus: To improve the rate of force development and intramuscular coordination

Procedure:

1. Assume a golf stance and anchor your elbows against your sides while holding the medicine ball.
2. Rotate as you would in backswing; then rotate in the opposite direction as if to hit a golf ball, releasing the medicine ball.

Volume: 5 to 10 repetitions in each direction

Tip: Be sure to keep your arms still and move the hip as fast as possible.

LOWER-BODY EXERCISES

BENCH JUMP

Focus: To improve the rate of force development and intramuscular coordination

Procedure:

1. Stand with one foot on a bench and the other foot on the ground.
2. Begin jumping back and forth over the bench, being sure to concentrate.
3. The foot landing on the bench will alternate with each jump.

Volume: 10 to 20 repetitions

Tip: Increase the speed only as you become more comfortable with the exercise.

SIDE BOX

Focus: To improve the rate of force development and intramuscular coordination

Procedure:

1. Stand to one side of a box with both feet on the ground.
2. Jump to the top of the box and off the other side.
3. Alternate back and forth.

Volume: 10 to 20 repetitions in each direction

Tip: Spend as little time as possible on the ground and on the box.

CLUB TRAINING—LONG RESPONSE

HEAVY BASEBALL SWING

Focus: To initiate the stretch-shortening cycle

Procedure:

1. Assume a batting stance. Take the bat to the back position and pause for one second.
2. Swing directly through an imaginary baseball on a level plane.
3. Repeat.

Volume: 10 to 20 repetitions

Tip: You can do this swing in both directions.

LIGHT GOLF SWING

Focus: To improve speed and golf-swing carryover

Procedure:

1. Use an implement that is a few ounces less than club weight or grip a golf club at the club head end.

2. Assume a golf stance. Take the club to the top of the backswing and pause for one second.

3. Swing through the ball as you normally would in a golf swing.

4. Repeat.

Volume: 2 × 10 to 12 repetitions

STANDARD GOLF SWING

Focus: To improve speed and golf swing carryover

Procedure: Use a regular golf club.

1. Assume the golf stance. Take a long backswing and pause for one second.
2. Swing through the ball as you normally would.
3. Repeat.

Volume: 2 × 10 to 12 repetitions

Tip: May be done on one leg or two legs.

CLUB TRAINING—SHORT RESPONSE

HEAVY BASEBALL SWING

Focus: To activate the stretch-shortening cycle

Procedure:

1. Stand in an upright position with a baseball bat or weighted club.
2. Start with the bat slightly in front of a level impact point (i.e., the impact point of a baseball).
3. Move the bat as fast as possible in a backward direction.
4. As soon as the bat moves beyond the impact point, stop it from moving any further and reverse direction.

Volume: 10 to 12 repetitions

Tips:

- You can do this in both directions.
- It is important not to substitute with other parts of the body.

LIGHT GOLF SWING

Focus: To activate the stretch-shortening cycle

Procedure:

Use an implement that weighs a few ounces less than club weight or hold a golf club at the club head end.

1. Stand in a golf stance.

2. Start with the implement slightly in front of the impact point.

3. Move the implement as fast as possible in backward direction.

4. As soon as it moves beyond the impact point, stop the implement from moving any further and reverse directions.

Volume: 2 × 10 to 12 repetitions

Tips:

- You can do this drill in both directions.

- It is important not to substitute with other parts of the body.

STANDARD GOLF SWING

Focus: To activate the stretch-shortening cycle

Procedure:

1. Assume a golf stance.
2. Using a regular golf club, start with the club slightly in front of impact point.
3. Move the club as fast as possible in a backward direction.
4. As soon as the club moves beyond the impact point, stop it from moving any further and reverse direction.

Volume: 2 × 10 to 12 repetitions

Tip: It is important not to substitute with other parts of the body.

THE NEXT STEP

The scientific community recognizes club head speed as a series of actions governed by the laws of physics and the applications of physiology. The teaching community views club head speed as the measurement responsible for creating distance during the golf shot. Both groups are looking at the same thing but from different ends of the performance spectrum. Complications can arise from common spinal conditions that could require postural adjustments during the stance position. Likewise, soft tissue restrictions could lead to compensating swing mechanics, and poor strength and flexibility could force the golfer to mentally play outside inherent physical limitations.

Lack of consistent swing component skills will result not only in frustration and discouragement, but also in physical breakdown or poor performance. When you understand the concept that a successful golf swing is an efficient coiling and uncoiling process around the stable trunk with a reproducible golf club whipping action and achieve this action through appropriate practice, you will undoubtedly improve your golf game.

CHAPTER 7

NUTRITION FOR GOLF ENERGY NEEDS

Like your local grocery store and restaurant, the dining rooms on the PGA Tour have changed drastically in the past decade. Foods that have been around for a long time remain on the menu, but many more choices are available for people who want to eat healthier fare. Fried chicken is countered by low-fat chicken salad, and ice cream sundaes have a counterpart in frozen yogurt. While athletes in many sports have been advised to eat more nutritious meals for better sports performance, golfers have generally paid little attention to dietary factors. Perhaps because golf is a slow-moving activity that does not tax the aerobic or anaerobic energy systems, the advantages of healthy eating habits have not been appreciated fully. On the other hand, traditional postgame 19th-hole indulgences were responsible for many players leaving the golf course in poorer condition than when they started their round.

You undoubtedly are aware that several previously overweight professionals have made major improvements in their tournament standings after losing weight and getting in shape. All golfers can benefit from better nutrition and proper hydration, however, because these factors play a significant role in energy availability and utilization. Over the course of a golf game, your nutritional preparation can definitely help or hurt your playing performance.

© Action Images

PGA Tour player and 1992 Masters Champion Fred Couples.

NUTRITIONAL OVERVIEW

Dietary habits significantly affect your body weight, body composition, and physical health. Because most Americans consume too many calories for their level of activity, about three out of four adults are overweight, predisposing them to various diseases and degenerative problems. You should be aware that excessive body fat increases your risk of heart disease, joint problems, diabetes, low back pain, and many types of cancer. Of course, extra fat also interferes with proper swing mechanics and optimum golf performance. Conversely, reducing excess fat weight through proper nutrition and sensible exercise can result in improved swing technique and reduced fatigue during your game.

Understanding the problem is only the first step in making lifestyle changes that can lead to a more desirable body weight and better golf performance. Eating for the purpose of lower golf scores is advisable from a health and performance perspective. In addition to keeping your weight down, you keep your accessible energy stores up throughout a full game of golf. The physical improvements that result from strength training will motivate some golfers to modify their eating habits to further enhance their playing abilities. Others might need specific nutrition programs that present daily menus and dietary information. An excellent resource in this area is *Nancy Clark's Sports Nutrition Guidebook*.

In addition to knowing how to count calories and determine the fat content of various foods, be aware that eating too little protein or calcium can lead to a weak musculoskeletal system and even osteoporosis. Insufficient iron in the diet can cause anemia, and excessive sodium intake contributes to hypertension. Of course, we want just the opposite to feel and function better both on and off the golf course.

Eating foods high in fiber, low in fats, and rich in vitamins and minerals is essential for optimum health and physical function as well as for disease prevention. Potassium, for example, which is abundant in bananas and cantaloupes, is involved in every muscle contraction. Vitamins A and C, found in many fruits and vegetables, are important antioxidants (nutritional bodyguards) that protect the body cells from potentially harmful chemical reactions.

While nutritional supplements can supply vitamins and minerals, dietitians recommend that such supplements not substitute for well-balanced diets that include a variety of vegetables, fruits, and whole grains, as well as lean meats and low-fat dairy products. Human nutrient requirements are too complex (and too little understood) to be adequately supported by pills, and only a varied and well-rounded diet can provide the proper foundation for optimum nutrition. You should be familiar with the food categories and daily servings recommended by the United States Department of Agriculture in the Food Guide Pyramid. You also should understand that a well-balanced diet is not the same as a low-calorie diet designed for losing weight. Be sure your physician or a registered dietitian approves any reduced-calorie diet.

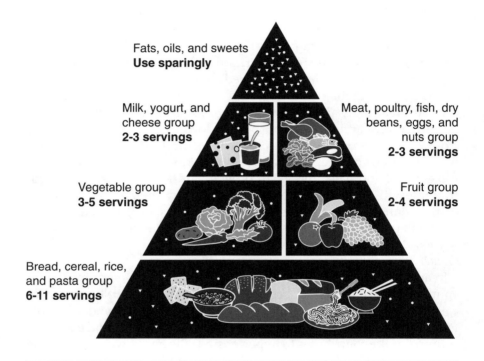

Food Guide Pyramid.

THE BASIC NUTRIENTS

The Food Guide Pyramid is high in carbohydrates, moderate in proteins, and low in fats. The carbohydrate choices are divided into grains, vegetables, and fruits. The suggested protein sources are low-fat milk products and lean meats, and the recommended fat-rich foods are vegetable oils (used sparingly). Let's consider each of the food categories more carefully.

Grains

Grains include all kinds of foods made from wheat, oats, corn, rice, and the like. Examples of grain foods are cereals, breads, pasta, pancakes, rice cakes, tortillas, bagels, muffins, cornbread, and rice pudding. Obviously, some flour-based foods such as cakes, cookies, and pastries contain a lot of fat, and should be eaten in moderation.

All grains are high in carbohydrates, and some (such as wheat germ) also are good sources of protein. Whole grains are typically rich in B vitamins and fiber. Grains are plentiful and inexpensive and should be part of every meal, from 6 to 11 servings every day. A serving is equivalent to a slice of bread or a half cup of pasta, so achieving the 6 to 11 servings should not be too difficult. Refer to table 7.1 for sample exchange units for popular food choices within the grains category.

Table 7.1 Exchange Units Equivalent to One Grain Serving

Cereals

> 1/4 c. nugget cereals (Grape Nuts)
> 1/3 c. concentrated bran cereals
> 1/2 c. cooked hot cereal (oatmeal or Cream of Wheat)
> 3/4 c. flaked cereals
> 1 1/2 c. puffed cereals

Breads

> 1/2 bagel or English muffin
> 1 slice bread
> 1 piece pita bread
> 1 tortilla

Grains

> 1/4 c. wheat germ
> 1/3 c. brown or white rice
> 1/2 c. pasta, macaroni, or noodles
> 1/2 c. hominy, barley, or grits

Snacks

> 3/4 oz. pretzels
> 3/4 oz. rice cakes
> 4 crackers (1 oz.)
> 3 c. air-popped popcorn

Vegetables

Like grains, vegetables are excellent sources of carbohydrates, vitamins, and fiber. Vegetables come in all sizes, shapes, colors and nutritional characteristics, and are relatively low in calories. Orange vegetables (e.g., carrots, sweet potatoes, winter squash) typically are good sources of vitamin A and beta-carotene. Green vegetables are characteristically high in vitamins B_2 and folic acid. Some of the many green vegetables are peas, beans, broccoli, asparagus, spinach, and lettuce. Red vegetables generally provide ample amounts of vitamin C. The best-known vegetables in this category are tomatoes and red peppers. Other vegetables are essentially white, at least under the skin. These include cauliflower, summer squash, potatoes, and radishes, many of which are good sources of vitamin C and potassium.

The Food Guide Pyramid recommends three to five daily servings of vegetables. One serving is one-half cup of any raw vegetable, except for lettuce and sprouts, which require one cup per serving. Because heating reduces water content, cooked vegetables require less space than uncooked vegetables and serving sizes may be smaller. Likewise, vegetable juices are more concentrated and require only one-half cup per serving.

It is a good idea to eat some vegetables raw, and to steam or microwave vegetables for nutrient retention. Also note that fresh and frozen vegetables have more nutritional value and are lower in sodium than canned vegetables.

Fruit

Fruits also are relatively low in calories, with just as much variety and nutritional value as vegetables. Essentially all fruit choices are high in carbohydrates and vitamins, and many provide excellent sources of fiber.

Citrus fruits, such as oranges, grapefruit, and lemons, are loaded with vitamin C. Like orange-colored vegetables, orange fruits—including cantaloupe, apricots, and papaya—are rich in vitamin A and beta-carotene. Green fruits (honeydew, melon, kiwi) and red fruits (strawberries, cherries) also are high in vitamin C. Yellow fruits (peaches, mangos, pineapples) usually are good sources of vitamin C. Fruits that are white on the inside (apples, pears, bananas) are high in potassium.

Dried fruit is particularly dense, and the natural sweetness makes it a healthy substitute for high-fat snacks such as candy bars. Raisins, dates, figs, and prunes are all superb energy sources, and prunes are the single best source of dietary fiber.

The Food Guide Pyramid recommends two to four servings of fruit every day. Table 7.2 presents sample exchange quantities for a variety of fruits. You will notice that one serving varies considerably depending on the type of fruit eaten. For example, it takes one-quarter of a melon or one-half of a grapefruit to equal three dates or two tablespoons of raisins. The difference is water content. Fresh fruit contains lots of water, whereas dried fruit is essentially a high-density carbohydrate. If you prefer fruit in liquid form, one-half cup of fruit juice equals one serving, but has less fiber than whole fruit.

Table 7.2   Exchange Units Equivalent to One Fruit Serving

2 T. raisins	1 pear	1/4 melon
3 dates	3 apricots	1/2 mango
3 prunes	1/2 grapefruit	5 kumquats
1/2 c. grapes	3/4 c. pineapple	1 c. honeydew
3/4 c. berries	2 kiwi	1 1/4 c. strawberries
1 apple	1/2 pomegranate	1 1/4 c. watermelon
1 banana	1/4 canteloupe	1/4 papaya
	1 peach	

Milk Products

The Food Guide Pyramid recommends two to three daily servings of low-fat dairy products, including milk, yogurt, and cheese. These foods are excellent sources of protein and calcium. Because whole milk products are high in fat, be selective at the dairy counter. For example, skim milk, 1-percent milk, low-fat yogurt, and nonfat cottage cheese offer heart-healthy alternatives to higher-fat dairy selections.

Table 7.3 shows exchange units equivalent to one dairy serving. Notice that one-quarter cup of low-fat cheese has similar nutrition value to one cup of 1-percent milk. Although there are many sources of dietary protein, you may have difficulty obtaining sufficient calcium unless you regularly consume milk products. If you have problems digesting milk (lactose intolerance), be sure to eat other foods that are high in calcium such as tofu, leafy greens, beans, broccoli, and sesame seeds.

Table 7.3   Exchange Units Equivalent to One Dairy Serving

1 oz. low-fat cheese	1/2 c. evaporated skim milk
1/4 c. low-fat or nonfat cottage cheese	1 c. nonfat or 1% milk
1/4 c. part-skim ricotta cheese	1 c. low-fat or nonfat yogurt
1/4 c. parmesan cheese	1 c. low-fat buttermilk

Meats

This category includes meat, poultry, fish, eggs, nuts, and dry beans. All are good sources of protein, although some also contain significant amounts of fat. Table 7.4 presents sample foods in the meat category according to their fat content. Note that how meat is prepared has a lot to do with how much fat it provides. This nutritional aspect will be presented in more detail in the food preparation section.

Table 7.4   Meat Group Foods Categorized by Fat Content

Low fat	Medium fat	High fat
All fish	Chicken with skin	Beef ribs
Egg whites	Turkey with skin	Pork ribs
Chicken without skin	Roast beef	Corned beef
Turkey without skin	Roast pork	Sausage
Venison	Roast lamb	Lunch meat
Rabbit	Veal cutlet	Ground pork
Top round	Ground beef	Hot dogs
Eye of round	Steaks	Fried chicken
Sirloin tenderloin	Canned salmon	Fried fish
Flank steak	Oil-packed tuna	Nuts
Veal	Whole eggs	Peanuts
Dry beans	Pork chops	Peanut butter

While there are differences in fat content, protein exchange units are quite consistent among the foods in the meat category. As you can see from table 7.5, three ounces of meat, poultry, and fish (about the size of a deck of cards) have equal exchange value, as do one-quarter cup of dry beans and one-quarter cup of tuna. Try to consume two to three servings from the meat group, for a total of six to nine ounces, on a daily basis.

Table 7.5   Exchange Units Equivalent to One Meat Serving

3 oz. fish	1 T. peanut butter
3 oz. poultry	1/4 c. cooked dry beans
3 oz. meat (beef, poultry, lamb, etc.)	1/4 c. tuna
1 egg or 2 egg whites	1/4 c. tofu

Fats

The smallest section of the Food Guide Pyramid is the fat group, which should be consumed sparingly. Although all fats contain over nine calories per gram, some fats are more desirable than others from a health perspective. For example, consuming saturated fats (such as those found in mayonnaise, butter, and sour cream) presents a higher risk for developing heart disease than consuming monounsaturated fats (such as those found in olive oil and canola oil) and polyunsaturated fats (such as those found in margarine and corn oil). See table 7.6 to determine serving equivalents for foods in the fat group.

As you are undoubtedly aware, fat consumption has become a major issue in mainstream America, with various authorities recommending different amounts of dietary fat intake. Whereas some cardiologists, such as Dr. Dean Ornish, advise that heart patients eat only 10 percent of daily calories from fat, the American Heart Association and the American Dietetic Association allow up to 30 percent fat calories in the daily diet. According to the American Council on Exercise, most athletic individuals should consume between 20 to 30 percent of their calories from fat. We agree with this recommendation, but prefer diets closer to 20 percent fat calories.

An excellent diet plan for golfers is Dr. James Rippe's *Exercise Exchange Program,* which provides about 23 percent fat, 23 percent protein, and 54 percent carbohydrate calories on a daily basis.

Table 7.6   Exchange Units Equivalent to One Fat Serving

1 t. butter	1 T. salad dressing
1 t. margarine	1 T. cream cheese
1 T. diet margarine	2 T. light cream cheese
1 t. mayonnaise	2 T. sour cream
1 T. diet mayonnaise	4 T. light sour cream
1 t. oil	2 T. coffee creamer (liquid)
2 T. diet salad dressing	

WATER: THE MOST IMPORTANT NUTRIENT

Water, though not included in the Food Guide Pyramid because it contains no calories and is not technically a food, is by far the most important human nutrient. The human body is mostly water (muscles are 80 percent water) and can survive only a few days without adequate hydration.

The standard recommendation is to consume eight 8-ounce glasses of water daily, but people who exercise need considerably more. Golfers who spend several hours in the sun during a game should drink at least four additional glasses of water. We suggest that you drink at least one glass of water before teeing off, and another glass every hour of play. This can easily be accomplished by carrying a quart-size water bottle in your golf bag or cart.

Because coffee, tea, diet drinks, and alcoholic beverages act as diuretics (which have a dehydrating effect), you should not count these in your daily water supply; but you may substitute beverages such as seltzer and fruit juices for water. Apple juice is an excellent source of potassium, and orange juice is high in vitamin C. Cranberry juice approaches orange juice in vitamin C content, and could help prevent bladder infections. Carrot juice is high in vitamin A, vitamin C, potassium, and fiber.

THREE STEPS TO BETTER NUTRITION

An eating program that provides all of the essential nutrients but limits fat consumption requires careful food selection, substitution, and preparation. The following suggestions should be useful for establishing more healthful eating habits.

Food Selection

If you follow the Food Guide Pyramid recommendations—emphasizing grains, vegetables, and fruit, along with moderate amounts of milk and meat products—your diet will be high in nutrition and low in fat. You should, however, be very selective in the fat category. Because saturated fats such as those found in butter, cream, egg yolks, palm oil, and coconut oil raise blood cholesterol levels, you should consume these food items sparingly. Instead, select monounsaturated fats (such as olive, canola, and peanut oils) or polyunsaturated fats (such as safflower, sunflower, and corn oils). Mono- and polyunsaturated oils tend to lower blood cholesterol levels and therefore might help reduce the risk of heart disease.

The following contain less saturated fat than other choices in their category and are preferred selections: fish; poultry without skin; low-fat milk, yogurt, and cottage cheese; olive, peanut, sunflower, safflower, corn, and canola oils.

Food Substitution

Most people have favorite foods they don't want to give up in spite of the fat content. The good news is that simple substitutions can reduce fat content without detracting from taste. For example, using evaporated skim milk in place of cream cuts fat and cholesterol content by more than 65 percent; and using plain nonfat yogurt or nonfat sour cream in place of sour cream on baked potatoes reduces cholesterol content by 90 percent—and supplies the body with twice as much beneficial calcium.

Other useful substitutes are two egg whites in place of a whole egg, herbs rather than table salt, low-fat frozen yogurt or ice milk instead of ice cream, cocoa powder in place of chocolate squares in baked goods, and lemon juice or vinegar instead of high-fat salad dressings.

If you have a sweet tooth, we suggest dried fruit (raisins, dates, figs, prunes, dried apricots) in place of candy, cookies, and fat-rich baked goods. If you prefer crunchy snacks like potato chips, consider lower-fat alternatives such as pretzels, baked chips, or carrot sticks.

Food Preparation

How food is prepared can increase or decrease the fat content. Frying can double and triple the calories in some foods. Using nonfat vegetable spray or a nonstick skillet can eliminate the fats and oils typically used for frying. It also is better to cook vegetables separate from meat so they won't absorb the meat fats. We suggest baked or broiled meats, and steamed or microwaved vegetables, for greatest retention of nutrients. Try not to add butter and salt to vegetables during cooking: It takes less salt and fat to make food taste good after cooking than during cooking.

FOOD FOR BUILDING MUSCLE

You might be concerned about obtaining enough energy for your workouts and golf games, as well as sufficient nutrients for building muscle and increasing your driving distance. Although the Food Guide Pyramid recommendations should be sufficient in all these areas, this section presents more specific information about the calorie and protein needs of golfers who strength-train. Strength training generally requires between 5 to 10 calories per minute during exercise performance. Completing a 25-minute circuit of resistance machines with little rest between successive exercises therefore burns approximately 125 to 250 additional calories.

Because of its vigorous nature, strength training leads to considerable post-exercise calorie utilization. Resting metabolic rate may remain about 10 percent higher than normal for more than an hour after a vigorous strength-training session.

In addition to these direct energy requirements, strength training produces more muscle and more active tissue, which consume calories all day long. At rest, a pound of muscle uses more than 35 calories every day just for tissue maintenance. Because golfers typically add three to four pounds of muscle after two months of strength training, their resting metabolism may require an additional 100 to 150 calories per day, every day of the week.

Golfers who do strength training might need to eat about 225 to 400 additional calories on their exercise days. Although this can be accomplished by consuming high-energy drinks, sports bars, or other food supplements, it is better to have additional servings from the Food Guide Pyramid. An extra serving each from the grains, fruits, vegetables, and milk groups should total between 225 and 400 calories, and also provide a variety of important nutrients. Of course, golfers who want to lose body weight might maintain their usual food intake or even reduce their calories slightly.

Another concern for golfers who strength-train is obtaining sufficient protein to build muscle tissue. Because muscle is 80 percent water, the more important factor is to maintain a high level of hydration, drinking at least eight glasses of water every day, and more on workout days. Although it is necessary to eat enough protein to facilitate muscle-building processes, the general protein recommendation of one gram for every two pounds of body weight is more than sufficient. In fact, researchers have consistently found no additional muscle-building benefit associated with consuming extra protein.

Using the guideline of one gram of protein for every two pounds of body weight, a female golfer who weighs 120 pounds should consume approximately 60 grams of protein daily. A 180-pound male golfer should eat approximately 90 grams of protein each day. For those who desire an extra margin of protein just to be sure, an additional serving of low-fat dairy products or lean meats should be more than adequate. Commercial protein supplements generally are unnecessary, but may be taken with a physician's or dietitian's approval. Just be sure that extra protein is accompanied by extra water to facilitate kidney function. Keep in mind that excessive protein consumption can reduce body/bone calcium content and overstress the kidneys as they attempt to excrete the nitrogen waste products associated with protein metabolism.

CARBOHYDRATES FOR HIGH-ENERGY GOLF GAMES

Because a golf game can take several hours to complete, you should be sure to eat plenty of carbohydrate foods in your daily meals. Carbohydrates, such as grains, vegetables, and fruits, are superb sources of energy, which is stored as glycogen in the muscles and liver. The rate at which carbohydrates raise blood sugar levels varies depending upon their glycemic response, however. Carbohydrates with a low glycemic index release sugars into the bloodstream slowly, maintaining elevated energy levels for a relatively long period of time. Conversely, carbohydrates with a high glycemic index release sugars into the bloodstream quickly, producing elevated energy levels for a relatively short period of time.

Golfers therefore should have a preround snack that emphasizes carbohydrates with a low glycemic index. These foods include apples, bananas, oranges, low-fat fruit yogurt, bran cereal, rice, and many types of food bars. In addition to providing a long-term energy source, these are healthful and nutritious foods that are easy to eat and digest.

If energy levels drop during a golf game, we recommend consuming high glycemic response carbohydrates to restore blood sugar levels quickly. Although bagels, graham crackers, vanilla wafers, and raisins are excellent choices, we prefer sports drinks with a high glycemic index (Gatorade, Powerade, etc.) or fruit juices. In addition to enhancing energy availability, sports drinks and fruit juices replenish fluids that can be easily depleted when golfing on hot or humid days. We also advise drinking plenty of fluids (water, fruit juices, and sports drinks) after the game to rehydrate the body.

THE NEXT STEP

Nutrition for golfers is basically the same as nutrition for all adults and athletes who desire good health and body composition. You should find that a sound eating program provides plenty of energy for your strength-training workouts and golf games, as well as the essential nutrients to enhance your muscle development and driving distance. We recommend the food categories and portions presented in the USDA's Food Guide Pyramid: 6 to 11 daily servings of grains, 3 to 5 daily servings of vegetables, 2 to 4 daily servings of fruit, 2 to 3 daily servings of milk products, 2 to 3 daily servings of meats, and small quantities of fats such as nuts and monounsaturated or polyunsaturated oils.

Golfers should drink up to 12 glasses of water on workout days and game days, and at least 8 glasses on nonexercise days. Energy requirements for 25 minutes of circuit strength training may be 125 to 250 calories, and the muscle-building effects of regular strength training may require a total of 225 to 400 extra calories on exercise days. Although additional calories may be necessary for golfers who strength-train, research does not reveal a need for extra protein (more than one gram of protein for every two pounds of body weight) if you follow the nutritional guidelines in the Food Guide Pyramid. We recommend eating a preround snack containing carbohydrates with low glycemic response, and consuming sports drinks or fruit juices during play to maintain high energy levels.

CHAPTER 8

COMPLETE GOLF CONDITIONING PROGRAM

The game of golf is changing by the proverbial leaps and bounds. The technology and teaching techniques have changed over the last 15 years to allow marginal players to become respectable in their abilities, respectable players to become good, and amateur players to become even better. It is now more evident than ever that a golfer needs to condition and train the body to improve the game. Many professional golfers, including Greg Norman, have hired professional physical therapists to travel and take care of both their rehabilitation and fitness needs. Tiger Woods, Mark O'Meara, Fred Couples, Tom Watson, Justin Leonard, and Brad Faxon have all hired physical therapists or conditioning specialists to design programs for them.

While you might not have the luxury of hiring your own personal trainer or personal physical therapist, you can improve your game just by committing two 15- to 20-minute sessions a week to a golf conditioning

Justin Leonard, one of the new breed of PGA Tour players.

program. Even if you live in a northern climate, you can take advantage of the four winter months to get ready for your golf season. What a wonderful way to stay involved with the game of golf, while committing yourself to better physical condition and improved playing performance next season! If you really want to become a good golfer, it is not necessary to strive for the muscularity of David Duval, the flexibility of Tiger Woods, the trunk strength of Greg Norman, or the sequencing of Tom Watson. It is more important to have discipline enough to do a few small things that can change your body—and your swing—for the better. Then you will really be able to improve your game.

PEAKING AT THE RIGHT TIME

Getting in shape for golf requires as little as two 15- to 20-minute exercise sessions per week. As your condition improves, however, your exercise time and effort can be progressively increased and integrated into a periodized training program in which you emphasize different conditioning components for various time periods throughout the year. Periodization training simply organizes your training for achieving a projected goal. More advanced, periodized training is not difficult to implement and should further enhance your physical development. The success of any training program is based on how you are able to control, modify, and manipulate two key variables: volume and intensity. The two components of periodization in essence state:

> As intensity increases, volume decreases.
> As volume increases, intensity decreases.

Always keep in mind that an increase in one factor requires a decrease in the other.

The key to manipulating these variables successfully is to listen to what your body is trying to tell you. To minimize your risk of injury, take a thorough medical, structural, and functional assessment before engaging in any exercise program (see chapter 2).

Begin formulating your golf program by finding the weak link of your swing and focusing on how to develop that area through joint flexibility (chapter 3), muscle strength (chapter 4), postural stability (chapter 5), or motor learning (chapter 6). Determining your weak link might require self-evaluation or an assessment by a teaching pro or medical professional (see chapter 2)

Most competitive golfers have planned training periods of preseason, in-season, postseason, and off-season. Professional players typically need to be at their very best at least four to five times per year, such as at the Players Championship, the Masters, the U.S. Open, the British Open, and the PGA Championship. Like you, top players focus their programs on aerobic capacity, flexibility, power, strength, motor learning, and skill practice. Certain aspects of their exercise program are emphasized during some periods, however, and others during other periods. In season, for example, a competitive golfer will want to focus on maintaining strength, power, and stabilization training while improving golf-specific skills on the course. A typical in-season training schedule for a competitive golfer might include three workouts per week:

Day 1:   Strength training performed first day after tournament.

Day 2:   Power training performed one to two days before or after tournament. The number of reps and weight of the medicine ball would be dictated by the time of year and the day of the week.

Day 3:   Posture training using the stabilization ball and tubing program. Work out on the day you play a morning round.

The recreational golfer, on the other hand, is likely to rely less on program design. We recommend recreational golfers participate in strength and flexibility exercises no less than twice per week:

Day 1:   Strength training and power training

Day 2:   Posture training with stabilization

WORKOUT PROGRESSION

As you've read throughout this book, total fitness involves many different components. Flexibility, strengthening, postural balance, and motor learning are several factors that can affect the golf swing. Different players require different training emphasis on each component for addressing their specific strengths and weaknesses. Proper training percentages of each component can be determined based on age, gender, physical status, period of season, and skill level. For example, a 55-year-old female golfer might emphasize strength development during her off-season, whereas a 25-year-old male golfer might emphasize flexibility exercises during his off-season. Although training has become more scientific, it still is basically uncomplicated in its fundamental application: If something is tight, stretch it; if something is weak, strengthen it; if something is clumsy, balance and coordinate it.

Once you have pinpointed the golf skills and performance links that you need to work on, determine your level of fitness and time available to train with one of the following four weekly workout schedules (tables 8.1 through 8.4). Level I workout weeks are great for beginning golfers who have just started training seriously for the sport, whereas level IV workout weeks are geared for the competitive player. If you are

Table 8.1   Level I

	Off-season	In season
Flexibility	3–5 × per wk (10 min)	3 × per wk (6 min)
Strength training	3 × per wk (10 min)	2 × per wk (8 min)
Lower body	2 × 20 reps	1 × 20 reps
Upper body	1 × 15 reps	1 × 15 reps
Trunk (day 1/day 2)	time/reps	time/reps
Balance	3 × per wk (5 min)	2 × per wk (5 min)
Skill training	2 × per wk (5 min)	2 × per wk (5 min)

Table 8.2   Level II

	Off-season	In season
Flexibility	3–5 × per wk (12 min)	3 × per wk (10 min)
Strength training	3 × per wk (15 min)	2 × per wk (8 min)
Lower body	3 × 20 reps	2 × 20 reps
Upper body	2 × 15 reps	1 × 15 reps
Trunk (day 1/day 2)	time/reps	time/reps
Balance	3 × per wk (5 min)	2 × per wk (5 min)
Skill training	2 × per wk (5 min)	2 × per wk (3 min)

planning to train year-round, you might want to start training at Level I and progress through Levels II and III, and end your season with Level IV.

Table 8.3   Level III

	Off-season	In season
Flexibility	4–5 × per wk (12 min)	4 × per wk (12 min)
Strength training	3–4 × per wk (15-20 min)	2 × per wk (12 min)
Lower body	3 × 20 reps	2 × 20 reps
Upper body	2 × 15 reps	2 × 15 reps
Trunk (day 1/day 2)	time/2 reps	time/2 reps
Balance	4 × per wk (5 min)	2 × per wk (5 min)
Skill training	3 × per wk (5 min)	4 × per wk (3–5 min)

Table 8.4   Level IV

	Off-season	In season
Flexibility	5–7 × per wk (15 min)	5 × per wk (12 min)
Strength training	3–4 × per wk (20–25 min)	2 × per wk (12–15 min)
Balance	4 × per wk (5–7 min)	2 × per wk (5 min)
Skill training	4 × per wk (5–7 min)	2 × per wk (3–5 min)

Warm-Up and Flexibility

Before any workout, it is important to perform breathing and relaxation exercises for 10 minutes to help you perfect your breathing and develop focus. Next, warm up your muscles with aerobic activities such as walking, climbing, biking, or swimming for 20 to 45 minutes. After the aerobic segment of your workout, take three to five minutes to focus again on your breathing and regulate it the remainder of the workout.

Once you've warmed up your muscles, start your flexibility exercises (see chapter 3) within a pain-free range.

Strength Training

Start the strength training segment of the program with a medicine ball warm-up to assist with weight-shifting maneuvers while maintaining trunk stability. Upper body, lower body, and trunk exercises are then performed for strengthening purposes.

The functional upper body program represents a more golf-specific training component. The purpose of the functional upper body program is to exercise your muscles through a full range of motion while avoiding shoulder joint irritation. This places the hands and arms in even more positions than are used during the golf swing. The result should be enhanced driving performance, because your conditioning drills cover all of the movement range in your swinging action.

Balance Training and Muscle Memory

Muscle memory exercises help to activate specific muscles. For example, because the rotator cuff must work to stabilize your swing regardless of how much weight is being lifted, it is important to always activate the rotator cuff. Don't perform the muscle memory exercise to fatigue or for the purpose of building strength. Rather, focus on becoming more aware of your muscles and how they are moving. Next, perform slide board slides so that the power center of the body, which includes the hips and gluteal muscles, can stabilize to provide a strong base for lifting with the lower body, especially when using dynamic exercises.

Stabilization Exercises

The purpose of the ball stabilization program is to incorporate trunk stability. As we have explained, trunk stability is essential during the golf swing so that proper spine position can be maintained throughout the entire action. The following exercises incorporate both lower- and upper-body strengthening activities, but the focus of the entire program is to make sure the trunk remains stable. Stretching can be repeated at the end of the program, if time permits. Address only the muscles that have been tight in the past or have potential for breakdown.

Greg Norman's Workout

The repetitive nature of the golf swing predisposes both the professional and amateur golfer to injury. The objective of any exercise program is to enhance performance as well as prevent injury.

Greg Norman's extensive business, golf, and travel schedules all can contribute to breakdown of his body. This is why he views fitness as a key component in his overall lifestyle. He alternates parts of these five exercise programs throughout the course of the year. In addition, we constantly evaluate ways of improving his programs.

We've provided six of Greg Norman's workouts to show you the basic format of a solid training session: aerobic activity to warm up the body and maintain cardiovascular conditioning, flexibility training, strength training (upper body, lower body, and trunk), balance training, and stabilization training (including muscle memory and power training). We've organized Greg's golf workouts (tables 8.5 through 8.10) so that you can maintain your physical conditioning all year long. The variety of the exercises in the programs help keep you interested in your conditioning.

Greg's programs train the neuromuscular system segmentally, focusing on the fitness components necessary for reproducing one successful swing after another. Those components include functional flexibility, golf-specific muscular strength, dynamic postural balance, and segmental coordination. There are several factors we consider when organizing his workout schedule:

- *Time of season.* Are we planning for in-season or off-season work? What are the major tournaments or tour stops on which we want to focus?

- *Time of week.* Is it the beginning of the week, pro/am day, moving day, or Sunday's last round?

- *Practice time available.* How much practice time is available each week given other commitments, travel time, etc.?

- *Volume versus intensity.* Is it the time of year when we want to build a strength base (typically the off-season) or do we want to create power (late in the off-season, or early in the season)?

- *Loaded versus unloaded.* We save loaded exercises for earlier in the workout and unloaded exercises for later in a workout or after the player has hit a lot of practice balls.

> - *Repetition versus isometric hold.* Do we have an injury that will be aggravated by movement or do we need to strengthen the muscle throughout the full range of motion?
> - *Current health status.* Is he fatigued after living through five time zones in two weeks, or is he injured or ill?
>
> Greg works on his breathing during all of his workouts. After his workouts we evaluate any problem areas and occasionally do breathing and relaxation techniques.

WORKOUT 1

Because it is the most demanding, try doing this exercise program on the first workout day of the week. You can include this workout during both playing and nonplaying weeks. The program includes 20 to 45 minutes of aerobic activity, flexibility training and warm-up exercises, medicine ball work for the abdominal and low back routine, and traditional strength training.

Choose one or more of the activities listed for a combined total of 20 to 30 consecutive minutes:

Versaclimber	Walking
Stationary bike	Rowing ergometer
Stair stepper	Slide board
Jogging	Cross-country ski machine

Flexibility

Exercise	Page #	Reps × duration
Seated low back and groin	42	2 × 10 to 12 seconds
Seated hamstring	43	2 × 10 to 12 seconds
Seated figure four	44	2 × 10 to 12 seconds
Seated crossover	45	2 × 10 to 12 seconds
Kneeling hip flexor	38	2 × 10 to 12 seconds
Quad stretch	39	2 × 10 to 12 seconds
Calf stretch	40	2 × 10 to 12 seconds
Pec neck	47	2 × 10 to 12 seconds

Muscle Memory

Exercises	Page #	Sets × reps
Rotator cuff isometrics (inward)	53	1 × 20
Rotator cuff isometrics (outward)	53	1 × 20

Medicine Ball Warm-Up

Exercise	Page #	Duration	Ball size
Wood chopping	127	repeat for 20 to 30 seconds	1 kg to 3 kg
Backward throw	128	repeat for 20 to 30 seconds	1 kg to 3 kg
Russian twist	129	repeat for 20 to 30 seconds	1 kg to 3 kg
Discus throw	130	repeat for 20 to 30 seconds	1 kg to 3 kg

Medicine Ball Workout

Exercise	Page #	Sets × reps	Ball size
Seated overhead throw	131	1 × 10	1 kg to 3 kg
Seated chest pass	132	1 × 10	1 kg to 3 kg
Diagonal	133	1 × 10	1 kg to 3 kg
Side pass	137	1 × 10	1 kg to 3 kg

Strength Training—Upper Body

Exercise	Page #	Sets × reps
Bench press	81	4 × 8 to 12
One-arm bent row	82	2 × 12
Lateral raise	83	2 × 12
Super pullover	70	2 × 12
Triceps extension	73	2 × 12
Biceps curl	72	2 × 12

Strength Training—Lower Body

Exercise	Page #	Sets × reps
Squat or leg press	65, 77	4 × 15
Dumbbell lunge	76	2 × 8 to 12
Dumbbell step-up	75	2 × 8 to 12
Leg extension	63	2 × 8 to 12
Leg curl	64	2 × 8 to 12
Hip internal rotation	189	1 set to exhaustion
Hip external rotation	189	1 set to exhaustion

Strength Training—Abdominal Muscles and Lower Back

Exercise	Page #	Sets
Leg push down	98	1 to 2 sets to substitution*
Knees to ceiling	104	1 to 2 sets to substitution
Solo twist	102	1 to 2 sets to substitution
Russian twist sit-up	102	1 to 2 sets to substitution
Cobra	100	1 to 2 sets to substitution
Back extension	78	1 to 2 sets to substitution
Back hyper	102	1 to 2 sets to substitution

*Substitution occurs when you begin to use other muscles than abdominal or lower back muscles during the exercise.

WORKOUT 2

This exercise program can be done during playing and nonplaying weeks. Greg usually performs this program on Tuesdays of playing weeks. It involves aerobic activity, flexibility and warm-up exercises, functional upper body work using tubing and body-weight resistance activity, and stabilization ball activities. Greg Norman also includes rehab modalities, such as massage, if necessary.

Choose one or more of the activities listed for a combined total of 20 to 45 consecutive minutes:

Versaclimber	Walking
Stationary bike	Rowing ergometer
Stair stepper	Slide board
Jogging	Cross-country ski machine

Flexibility

Exercise	Page #	Reps × duration
Seated low back and groin	42	2 × 10 to 12 seconds
Seated hamstring	43	2 × 10 to 12 seconds
Seated figure four	44	2 × 10 to 12 seconds
Seated crossover	45	2 × 10 to 12 seconds
Kneeling hip flexor	38	2 × 10 to 12 seconds
Quad stretch	39	2 × 10 to 12 seconds
Calf stretch	40	2 × 10 to 12 seconds
Pec neck	47	2 × 10 to 12 seconds

Muscle Memory

Exercises	Page #	Sets × reps
Rotator cuff isometrics (inward)	53	1 × 20
Rotator cuff isometrics (outward)	53	1 × 20

Medicine Ball Warm-Up

Exercise	Page #	Duration	Ball size
Wood chopping	127	repeat for 20 to 30 seconds	1 kg to 3 kg
Backward throw	128	repeat for 20 to 30 seconds	1 kg to 3 kg
Standing Russian twist	129	repeat for 20 to 30 seconds	1 kg to 3 kg
Discus throw	130	repeat for 20 to 30 seconds	1 kg to 3 kg

Functional Upper Body Program*

1. Keep your shoulder height level.
2. Be controlled and conscious of your form.
3. Go from one exercise directly to the next.
4. Exhale during lifting movements and inhale during lowering movements.

Exercise	Page #	Sets × reps	Comments
One-arm bent row	82	2 × 5	5 palm to thigh/5 palm facing
Bench press	81	3 × 5	5 palm down/5 thumb up/5 palm up
Lateral raise	83	2 × 5	5 palm up/5 palm down
Seated chop	107	1 × 15	
Triceps extension	73	1 × 15	Greg substitutes triceps throwback
Supine press	187	2 × 5	Greg does military press—5 palm forward/5 palm facing
Chest crossover	69	3 × 5	Greg does shoulder crosses—5 palm down/5 thumb up/5 palm up
Push up		2 × 5	5 hands neutral/5 hands out at 45°
Super pullover	70	2 × 8	8 pull ups/8 chin ups; Greg substitutes Smith Machine
Triceps extension	73	1 × 10	Greg substitutes a dip exercise here
Cable archer		2 × 10	10 each way

*Greg also performs 15 traditional PNF pattern exercises called "Travoltas" in his upper body program. A PT can show you how to do such an exercise.

Strength Training—Lower Body*

Exercise	Page #	Sets and reps
Wall sit	185	2 × 12 (hold each rep 5 seconds)
Dumbbell lunge	76	2 × 8 to 12
Leg extension	63	2 × 8 to 12
Leg curl	64	2 × 8 to 12
Side box	138	2 × 8 to 12
Step up	75	2 × 8 to 12
Hip internal rotation	189	1 set to exhaustion
Hip external rotation	189	1 set to exhaustion

*Program developed in consultation with Dave Bailey and Tom House.

WORKOUT 3

This program includes easy, low-impact aerobic activity, flexibility, and an unloaded abdominal/low back routine. Use this program following several days of hard work and practice because it allows you to get your necessary muscular work in an unloaded and less stressful manner.

Choose one or more of the activities listed for a combined total of 30 to 40 consecutive minutes:

Swimming   Cycling
Hiking   Kayaking

Flexibility

Exercise	Page #	Reps × duration
Seated low back and groin	42	2 × 10 to 12 seconds
Seated hamstring	43	2 × 10 to 12 seconds
Seated figure four	44	2 × 10 to 12 seconds
Seated crossover	45	2 × 10 to 12 seconds
Kneeling hip flexor	38	2 × 10 to 12 seconds
Quad stretch	39	2 × 10 to 12 seconds
Calf stretch	40	2 × 10 to 12 seconds
Pec neck	47	2 × 10 to 12 seconds

Muscle Memory

Exercises	Page #	Sets × reps
Rotator cuff isometrics (inward)	53	1 × 20
Rotator cuff isometrics (outward)	53	1 × 20

Medicine Ball Warm-Up

Exercise	Page #	Duration	Ball size
Wood chopping	127	repeat for 20 to 30 seconds	1 kg to 3 kg
Backward throw	128	repeat for 20 to 30 seconds	1 kg to 3 kg
Standing Russian twist	129	repeat for 20 to 30 seconds	1 kg to 3 kg
Discus throw	130	repeat for 20 to 30 seconds	1 kg to 3 kg

Medicine Ball Workout

Exercise	Page #	Sets and reps	Ball size
Seated overhead throw	131	1 × 10	1 kg to 3 kg
Seated chest pass	132	1 × 10	1 kg to 3 kg
Diagonal	133	1 × 10	1 kg to 3 kg
Side pass	137	1 × 10	1 kg to 3 kg

WORKOUT 4

This program lasts only 45 to 60 minutes, but is very intense. The training circuit includes Versaclimber, bike, stair climbing, slide board, jump rope, boxing drills, hurdle drills, tubing exercises, medicine ball, and postural drills.

Choose one or more of the cardiorespiratory activities listed for a combined total of 20 to 30 consecutive minutes:

Versaclimber   Walking
Stationary bike   Rowing ergometer
Stair stepper   Slide board
Jogging   Cross-country ski machine

Flexibility

Exercise	Page #	Reps × duration
Seated low back and groin	42	2 × 10 to 12 seconds
Seated hamstring	43	2 × 10 to 12 seconds
Seated figure four	44	2 × 10 to 12 seconds
Seated crossover	45	2 × 10 to 12 seconds
Kneeling hip flexor	38	2 × 10 to 12 seconds
Quad stretch	39	2 × 10 to 12 seconds
Calf stretch	40	2 × 10 to 12 seconds
Pec neck	47	2 × 10 to 12 seconds

Muscle Memory

Exercises	Page #	Sets × reps
Rotator cuff isometrics (inward)	53	1 × 20
Rotator cuff isometrics (outward)	53	1 × 20

Medicine Ball Warm-Up

Exercise	Page #	Duration	Ball size
Wood chopping	127	repeat for 20 to 30 seconds	1 kg to 3 kg
Backward throw	128	repeat for 20 to 30 seconds	1 kg to 3 kg
Standing Russian twist	129	repeat for 20 to 30 seconds	1 kg to 3 kg
Discus throw	130	repeat for 20 to 30 seconds	1 kg to 3 kg

Functional Upper Body Program*

1. Keep your shoulder height level.
2. Be controlled and conscious of your form.
3. Go from one exercise directly to the next.
4. Exhale during lifting movements and inhale during lowering movements.

Exercise	Page #	Sets × reps	Comments
One-arm bent row	82	2 × 5	5 palm to thigh/5 palm facing
Bench press	81	3 × 5	5 palm down/5 thumb up/5 palm up
Lateral raise	83	2 × 5	5 palm up/5 palm down
Seated chop	107	1 × 15	
Triceps extension	73	1 × 15	Greg substitutes triceps throwback
Supine press	187	2 × 5	Greg does military press—5 palm forward/5 palm facing
Chest crossover	69	3 × 5	Greg does shoulder crosses—5 palm down/5 thumb up/5 palm up
Push up		2 × 5	5 hands neutral/5 hands out at 45°
Super pullover	70	2 × 8	8 pull ups/8 chin ups; Greg substitutes Smith Machine

continued

Exercise	Page #	Sets × reps	Comments
Triceps extension	73	1 × 10	Greg substitutes a dip exercise here
Cable archer		2 × 10	10 each way

*Greg also performs 15 traditional PNF pattern exercises called "Travoltas" in his upper body program. A PT can show you how to do such an exercise.

Strength Training—Lower Body*

Exercise	Page #	Sets and reps
Wall sit	185	2 × 12 (hold each rep 5 seconds)
Dumbbell lunge	76	2 × 8 to 12
Leg extension	63	2 × 8 to 12
Leg curl	64	2 × 8 to 12
Side box	138	2 × 8 to 12
Step up	75	2 × 8 to 12
Hip internal rotation	189	1 set to exhaustion
Hip external rotation	189	1 set to exhaustion

*Program developed in consultation with Dave Bailey and Tom House.

Strength Training—Abdominal Muscles and Lower Back

Exercise	Page #	Sets
Leg push down	98	1 to 2 sets to substitution*
Knees to ceiling	104	1 to 2 sets to substitution
Solo twist	102	1 to 2 sets to substitution
Russian twist sit-up	102	1 to 2 sets to substitution
Cobra	100	1 to 2 sets to substitution
Back extension	78	1 to 2 sets to substitution
Back hyper	102	1 to 2 sets to substitution

*Substitution occurs when you begin to use other muscles than abdominal or lower back muscles during the exercise.

WORKOUT 5

Due to demands placed on Greg Norman's time when he is on the road, it is important to develop a routine that is time-efficient, effective, portable, and progressive. This program is quite short and can be done in the privacy of a hotel room.

Choose one or more of the activities listed for a combined total of 20 consecutive minutes:

Versaclimber	Walking
Stationary bike	Rowing ergometer
Stair stepper	Slide board
Jogging	Cross-country ski machine

Flexibility

Exercise	Page #	Reps × duration
Seated low back and groin	42	2 × 10 to 12 seconds
Seated hamstring	43	2 × 10 to 12 seconds
Seated figure four	44	2 × 10 to 12 seconds
Seated crossover	45	2 × 10 to 12 seconds
Kneeling hip flexor	38	2 × 10 to 12 seconds
Quad stretch	39	2 × 10 to 12 seconds
Calf stretch	40	2 × 10 to 12 seconds
Pec neck	47	2 × 10 to 12 seconds

Muscle Memory

Exercises	Page #	Sets × reps
Rotator cuff isometrics (inward)	53	1 × 20
Rotator cuff isometrics (outward)	53	1 × 20

Medicine Ball Warm-Up

Exercise	Page #	Duration	Ball size
Wood chopping	127	repeat for 20 to 30 seconds	1 kg to 3 kg
Backward throw	128	repeat for 20 to 30 seconds	1 kg to 3 kg
Standing Russian twist	129	repeat for 20 to 30 seconds	1 kg to 3 kg
Discus throw	130	repeat for 20 to 30 seconds	1 kg to 3 kg

Medicine Ball Workout

Exercise	Page #	Sets × reps	Ball size
Seated overhead throw	131	1 × 10	1 kg to 3 kg
Seated chest pass	132	1 × 10	1 kg to 3 kg
Diagonal	133	1 × 10	1 kg to 3 kg
Side pass	137	1 × 10	1 kg to 3 kg

Ball Stabilization

Exercise	Page #	Sets × reps
Wall sit	185	1 × 20
Tubing back extension	106	1 × 15
Supine press	187	1 × 20
Back hypers	102	1 × 30
Tubing abduction	188	1 × 20
Wheelbarrow	105	15 × 55
Bridging	195	1 × 20
Lateral glide	109	1 × 10
Hamstring	35	2 × 20
Push up		2 × 20

WORKOUT 6

This workout is ideal before colder weather rounds or early tee-times. This short workout primarily aims to raise body temperature and improve dynamic flexibility.

Do 5 minutes of aerobic activity such as cycling, exercising on a versaclimber, or walking briskly.

Flexibility

Exercise	Page #	Reps × duration
Seated low back and groin	42	2 × 10 to 12 seconds
Seated hamstring	43	2 × 10 to 12 seconds
Seated figure four	44	2 × 10 to 12 seconds
Seated crossover	45	2 × 10 to 12 seconds
Kneeling hip flexor	38	2 × 10 to 12 seconds
Quad stretch	39	2 × 10 to 12 seconds
Calf stretch	40	2 × 10 to 12 seconds
Pec neck	47	2 × 10 to 12 seconds

Medicine Ball Warm-Up

Exercise	Page #	Duration	Ball size
Wood chopping	127	repeat for 20 to 30 seconds	1 kg to 3 kg
Backward throw	128	repeat for 20 to 30 seconds	1 kg to 3 kg
Standing Russian twist	129	repeat for 20 to 30 seconds	1 kg to 3 kg
Discus throw	130	repeat for 20 to 30 seconds	1 kg to 3 kg

THE NEXT STEP

The basic exercise program is an effective and efficient means for achieving a relatively high level of physical fitness and performance power. For further improvements in both areas, you might prefer a periodized training program. If nothing else, it adds variety and interest to your exercise program. The progressive and more-specialized approach of a well-designed periodization program ideally should result in peak fitness and golf performance during your most important matches. This type of training also should provide a comprehensive physical base from which to build a variety of skill drills and specific preparatory activities for a successful golf season.

CHAPTER 9

THE 15-MINUTE GOLF FITNESS WORKOUT

This program has been designed for

the recreational player who is unable to commit large amounts of time to training, but realizes some benefits that can be gained from a brief training session. Greg Norman uses this program when he is on the road. Many times, particularly when traveling overseas, you are not certain what type of training environment you might find. Because you might be on the road for as long as two to four weeks at a time, lack of regular strength and conditioning activities could lead to losing some of the fitness gains that were made in the preceding three months. It therefore is essential to have a time-efficient training program that does not require much equipment, is portable, and can be performed in the privacy of your hotel room.

SportsChrome East West/© Robert Tringali Jr.

Greg Norman sees fitness as an integral part of his everyday lifestyle.

The *15-minute golf fitness workout* serves this purpose perfectly and also is highly recommended for someone who has not previously participated in a fitness program specifically for golf. It addresses all components required to make positive changes in your body and your golf game. Remember, though, that you should not start an exercise program without an examination by a physician or qualified health care provider. Once you have the medical okay, you are ready to begin.

Most recreational golfers are not willing to spend long hours improving their fitness level. We live in a quick-fix society. That's why we've designed a time-limited program to train the neuromuscular system, enhance performance, and prevent injury (see table 9.1). This program not only satisfies golfers' playing needs, but trains for sport-related muscular strength, functional flexibility, dynamic postural balance, and segmental coordination. Strength exercises address the trunk, upper body, and lower body, while flexibility training focuses on the hips and low back.

Balance activities are basic; the two segmental sequencing drills are meant to create sequential separation and connection among the hips, trunk, and upper body. Try to do the program outlined below twice per week, but you may do any part of it (except the strength exercises) as often as you like.

Table 9.1   15-Minute Workout

Program component	Body focus	Exercise	Page #	Reps × duration
Flexibility	Hips and gluteals	Figure four	36	1 × 20 s
	Hip abductors	Crossover	37	1 × 20 s
	Abdominals & back	Double leg crossover	184	1 × 20 s
	Hamstrings	Seated hamstring	43	3 × 5 s
	Upper back	Seated club lat	46	5 × 3 s
	Abdominals	Press up	184	8 × 2 s
	Hip flexors	Standing hip flexor	48	1 × 20 s
	Hips, abdominals, & shoulders	Bow bend	50	1 × 20 s
Strength	Trunk	Abdominal hollowing	96	10 × 2 s
	Trunk	Prone leg raise	97	10 × 2 s
	Lower body	Wall sit	185	10 × 3-5 s
	Lower body	Bridging	186	10 × 3-5 s
	Upper body	Supine press	187	10 reps
	Upper body	Seated chop	107	10 reps each way
	Upper body	Seated lift	108	10 reps each way
Balance	Hip abductors	Tubing abductors	188	1 × 30 s each way
	Hip adductors	Tubing adductors	188	1 × 30 s each way
Segmental sequencing	Abdominals and lower back	Hip-trunk separation	192	30 s
	Abdominals and lower back	Hip-trunk separation & connection	193	30 s

DOUBLE LEG CROSSOVER

Focus: Abdominals and upper and lower back muscles

Procedure:

1. Lie on the floor on your left side with your knees pulled toward your chest. The knees should be pulled up as far as comfortable, at least to waist level if possible.

2. As you keep your knees still, supported, and anchored by one hand, roll your opposite shoulder backward toward the floor. Be sure to keep your right elbow close to the side of your body.

3. Hold this position for 20 seconds.

4. Return to the starting position and repeat on other side.

Tip: When you do the other side of the body, be sure that you roll the entire body over; don't just roll the legs over and keep your body on the other side.

PRESS UP

Focus: Midsection and abdominal muscles. The exercise is a passive movement to create muscle extension.

Procedure:

1. Lie face down on the floor. Place a pillow under the abdomen for support, if necessary.

2. If resting on your elbows is as high as you can go, begin in that position. If you are unable to raise your body off of the floor more than a few inches, this is your initial exercise position.

3. Initiate the movement by pressing up onto the elbows and allowing the hips to fall toward the ground.

4. Hold for 2 seconds and relax and repeat 8 times.

Tips:

- Be sure to use your arms, rather than your back muscles to hold yourself up.

- Controlled inhaling and exhaling should allow the pelvis to relax toward the floor as you press up. You should not feel discomfort.

WALL SIT

Focus: Quadriceps and hamstrings

Procedure:

1. Stand with your back facing the wall and feet approximately shoulder-width apart.

2. Place the stabilization ball between the middle of your back and the wall so that it is supported by the wall and your body.

3. Keeping the ball supported by the wall and your body, bend your knees as if you are sitting into a chair. Keep your shoulders back and maintain a slight curve in the lower spine such that the buttocks roll under the stabilization ball.

4. Sit to a comfortable level, but no deeper than having the backs of your thighs parallel to the ground.

5. Hold each sit for 3 to 5 seconds.

6. Return to the starting position.

Volume: 10 repetitions

BRIDGING

Focus: Gluteal, hamstring, and lower back muscles

Procedure:

1. Place the stabilization ball against a wall or other immovable surface.
2. Sit on the floor so that your back and shoulders rest against the ball.
3. Bend your knees and cross your arms in front of your chest.
4. Lay your head back so that your upper body weight rests on your shoulders.
5. In a slow and controlled manner, raise your buttocks from the floor, tighten, and hold.
6. Rest with your weight on your shoulders and with your body parallel to the ground. Be sure your hips remain level with one another throughout the exercise.
7. Hold for 3 to 5 seconds.
8. Return to the starting position.

Volume: 10 repetitions

Tip: Keep your weight on your shoulders and not your head or neck.

SUPINE PRESS

Focus: Chest, triceps, abdominal muscles, and shoulder external rotators

Procedure:

1. Lie flat on your back.

2. Position your feet on the floor closest to the anchoring spot of the tubing. You may place a towel under your head if it is extending back into the floor.

3. Pull your knees up toward your chest until the small of the back flattens against the floor.

4. Grasp the stirrups of the tubing with your hands, keeping your arms about eight inches away from your side.

5. While grabbing the stirrups, rotate the backs of your forearms so they move in the direction of the floor.

6. Slide your arms up along the floor until your elbows are at shoulder level. Be sure to keep the small of your back flat against the floor. You may raise your arms higher if your back remains flat.

7. Return to the starting position.

Volume: 10 repetitions

BALANCE

SINGLE LEG ABDUCTION AND ADDUCTION

Focus: Hip abductors and adductors

Procedure:

1. Attach the tubing to a door or fixed point on a wall and place the belt around your waist.

2. Standing parallel to the wall, walk outward from it, creating tension in the tubing.

3. Balancing on your inner leg, lift your outer leg off the ground.

4. Raise the inner leg off the ground and attempt to support on the outside leg.

5. Return to the starting position so that the tubing is at minimal tension and you are able to balance with both feet on the ground.

Duration: 30 seconds on each side

Tip: When you are working the leg farthest from the tubing attachment point, you may have to move in a little bit; those muscles may be a little bit weaker than the muscles used for supporting on the inside leg. They should be able to work well within a few weeks, however.

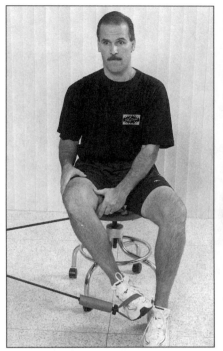 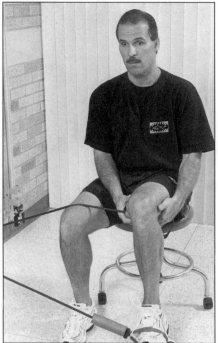

INTERNAL AND EXTERNAL HIP ROTATION

Focus: Hip abductors and adductors

Procedure:

1. Attach one end of the tubing to a door or fixed point on a wall and hold the other end.

2. Sit in a chair parallel to the wall and move away from the wall, creating tension in the tubing.

3. Place your end of the tubing around the foot closest to the wall.

4. Supporting your thigh with both hands, pull the leg away from the wall in a slow controlled manner.

5. Now place your end of the tubing around the foot farthest from the wall.

6. Supporting your thigh with both hands, pull this leg away from the wall in a slow controlled manner.

7. Turn the chair around 180 degrees and repeat for each leg.

Duration: 30 seconds for each leg on each side

TUBING RESISTIVE LUNGE

Focus: Hip flexor, hamstring, trunk, and gluteal muscles

Procedure:

1. Attach the tubing to a door or fixed point on a wall and place the belt around your waist.

2. Facing the wall, walk outward from it until you create tension in the tubing.

3. With your hands on your hips, step forward with one leg and lunge toward the wall being sure your front knee and lower leg are perpendicular to the floor.

4. Return to your starting position.

5. Repeat with opposite leg stepping forward.

Volume: 10 repetitions each leg

TUBING ASSISTIVE LUNGE

Focus: Hip flexor, hamstring, trunk, and gluteal muscles

Procedure:

1. Attach the tubing to a door or fixed point on a wall and place the belt around your waist.

2. Turn away from the wall and walk outward from it, creating tension in the tubing.

3. With your hands on your hips, step forward with one foot to lunge away from the wall. Be sure your front knee and lower leg are perpendicular to the floor.

4. Return to the starting position.

5. Repeat with opposite leg stepping forward.

Volume: 10 repetitions each leg

SEGMENTAL SEQUENCING

HIP-TRUNK SEPARATION

Focus: Abdominal and lower back muscles. This exercise attempts to disassociate the lower body from the upper body, which is needed to create separation in the golf swing.

Procedure:

1. Assume a golf stance in front of a mirror.

2. Place your hands across your chest.

3. Rotate your upper body backward, loading on the back leg and being sure you are hinging at the hips and not bending at the back.

4. Keep the upper body in the backswing position as you rotate your hips to initiate the forward swinging movement.

5. Return to the starting position and repeat.

Duration: 30 seconds

Tip: This exercise should not cause discomfort. Begin in an upright position and progress to the most comfortable golf stance position.

HIP-TRUNK SEPARATION AND CONNECTION

Focus: Abdominals and lower back muscles. This exercise will help create movement recall, which is needed for consistently reproducing the golf swing.

Procedure:

1. Assume a golf stance in front of a mirror with hands across your chest.

2. Rotate your upper body backward, loading on the back leg.

3. Keep the upper body in the backswing position as you rotate your hips to initiate the motion of swinging forward.

4. Now transfer your weight from your back foot to the front foot and turn your hips toward the target.

5. The front of your body should face the target, with weight rolled onto the left foot and the toes of the right foot, as your main support on the ground.

6. Return to the starting position and repeat.

Duration: 30 seconds

Tips:

- Try this exercise with a basketball or medicine ball in your hands.

- Be sure to hinge at your hips rather than bending at the back.

THE NEXT STEP

This 15-minute golf fitness workout offers a time-efficient approach to conditioning that addresses the essential components of joint flexibility, muscular strength, and dynamic postural balance. Although relatively brief, this specifically designed exercise program provides an excellent overall conditioning effect and is ideal for the time-pressured golfer. We do not recommend, however, that you limit your physical training to the 15-minute golf fitness workout. Do your best to follow the more comprehensive exercise programs presented in this book. Use this simplified workout as a substitute when your training time is limited; by doing so you should experience progressive improvement in both physical fitness and golf performance without missing scheduled training sessions.

ABOUT THE AUTHORS

One of the first conditioning experts to begin training golfers like athletes, **Pete Draovitch** has been personal physical therapist for PGA Tour star Greg Norman since 1993. He also serves as physical therapist and wellness consultant for Martin Memorial Medical Center, as president and CEO of The Bodyguards, Inc., and as spring training physical therapy consultant for the St. Louis Cardinals baseball organization.

An accomplished writer, Draovitch has had articles appear in *GOLF Magazine*, *Muscle Training in Orthopedics and Sports*, *Physical Therapy*, and numerous other publications. He has been featured in golf segments on ESPN, NBC High Performance Golf, and 60 Minutes and in articles in *GOLF Magazine*, *Sports Illustrated*, *Esquire*, and *USA Today*.

Draovitch holds a master's degree in physical therapy from the University of Miami and a master's degree in sports medicine/physical education from the University of Delaware. He is a member of the American Physical Therapy Association, the National Athletic Trainers' Association, and the National Strength and Conditioning Association.

With more than 35 years in strength training as an athlete, coach, teacher, professor, researcher, writer, and speaker, **Wayne Westcott**, PhD, is recognized as a leading authority on fitness. He has served as a strength training consultant for numerous organizations and programs, including Nautilus, the President's Council on Physical Fitness and Sports, the National Sports Performance Association, the International Association of Fitness Professionals (IDEA), the American Council on Exercise, the YMCA of the USA, and the National Youth Sports Safety Foundation.

He has received three of the highest honors in the fitness profession: the IDEA Lifetime Achievement Award in 1993, the President's Council Healthy American Fitness Leader Award in 1995, and the YMCA Robers-Gulick Memorial Award in 1998.

Westcott is currently the fitness research director at the South Shore YMCA in Quincy, Massachusetts, where he has carefully studied the physiological responses of adults to various programs of strength exercise. In 1996 he conducted a landmark study of 1,132 subjects showing that men and women over age 50 build strength and develop muscle at the same rate as younger adults. Together with co-author Tom Baechle, he wrote *Strength Training Past 50*, which was ranked as one of the ten best health and fitness books of 1997.

Westcott has authored ten other books on strength training, including *Building Strength and Stamina* and *Strength Fitness: Physiological Principles and Training Techniques*. He has published over 300 articles in professional fitness journals and has written a weekly fitness column for one of Boston's largest newspapers since 1986. He has served on the editorial boards of *Prevention, Shape, Men's Health, Fitness, Club Industry, American Fitness Quarterly,* and *Nautilus*.

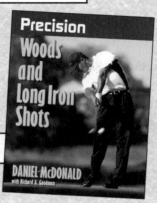